Our Country!

A Celebration of America in Words and Pictures

By the Editors of
U.S.News & World Report Books

Published by the
Book Division, U.S.News & World Report, Inc.
Washington, D.C.

Books by
U.S.News &
World Report

Joseph Newman
Directing Editor

A division of
U.S.News &
World Report, Inc.
Washington, D.C.

Library of Congress
Catalog Card Number 79-181532
Printed in the
United States of America

Project Editor
Ruth Adams Paepcke

Art Director
Donald McCarten

Picture Editor
Maria Ealand

Contributing Writer
Harry W. Baehr

Contents

Introduction *by Archibald MacLeish*

Back in the Nineteen Sixties someone remarked that the American young seemed to think the history of the Republic began with the inauguration of John Kennedy. It was a reasonably accurate observation: for some years a whole American generation talked about the United States as though it were a foreign country, recently—only recently—visited by intelligent human beings. The situation in the Seventies is not radically different. The young are more sophisticated, though courses in American history are still said to be scantily attended, and stories are told of reasonably intelligent boys and girls who can't place Adolf Hitler. But ground has been lost at other levels. If the know-nothing young are fewer than they were a decade ago, the general indifference to the American past, bewilderment about the American present and apprehension for the American future is, if anything, greater than it was. The much discussed young have been joined in their skepticism by whole categories of the middle-aged who, as the political behavior of the country indicates, will vote for anyone so long as the vote can be said to register a protest. And as for the old, they have begun to gather in colonies in sunny corners of the Republic where their principal activity, next to shuffleboard, is a ritual wringing of the hands.

The complaint at all ages is much the same, though it tends to lose its specifics as the age goes up. To the middle-aged and the old it is enough to observe, with or without adjectives, that the country has gone to Hell. To the young, fresh from the instruction of the philosophers of the New Left, the trouble lies deeper: the trouble is not that the country has gone to Hell but that it was conceived in that climate. Thomas Jefferson was a bourgeois intellectual. John Locke was a philosopher who had never read Marx. The American Proposition is a relic of Eighteenth Century ignorance. And when Abraham Lincoln talked about The People he had no idea what the word meant: he had never heard of the proletariat.

You can laugh. You should laugh: nothing quite as comical as the New-Left fables about the United States has turned up since Mr. Dooley. But when it comes to the feelings under the fables there is less to be amused about. Take a pleasant old couple from Iowa retired into the brassy fog of Los Angeles and trying to get along on an annuity bought with the sweat of their working years. When *they* say the Republic has gone to Hell it's a very real Hell they have in mind, not a professional fantasy. Where, they want to know, is the United States of America they used to hear about: a country where people could live and work in peace? And what is this other country—cities where you can't even walk on the streets and old women are knocked into gutters by teen-aged kids and robbed and kicked at and the Mafiosi murder each other and anyone else they please next door to the police station? And all these people talking about rotting cities and reeking rivers and poisoned air—is it the New World they mean or, if not, where has the New World gone to? They go on like that on the front porch in Los Angeles with the stucco cracking at their backs and the sunset jaundiced with smog to the westward, and nobody answers them. And they go off to bed at last, bewildered and afraid.

It isn't a question of what the Joe McCarthys used to call "loyalty" twenty-five years ago. Even the revolutionaries are "loyal" now. Oh, they talk about revolution on the Left but they never define what they mean—maybe a plot to kidnap Henry Kissinger—and as for the Far Right, they never produce a scheme for dismantling the Constitution without wrapping it up in the flag. Nevertheless, loyalty or not, the feel of the country has changed. You can put it bluntly. The old unquestioning love of the Republic is a rare thing these days. No man in public life feels about the country as Webster felt or Lincoln. We have our patrioteers whom we know how to value, but when it comes to talk about the apprehensions and anxieties which afflict us all, no one talks to us as Webster would have talked. No one speaks of the greatness of the Republic, its human greatness, its hope, its struggle. They tell us instead that nothing is really wrong—that the trouble is all in the newspapers or, worse still, in the wicked commentators on TV. There's nothing wrong with the country, we're told, that wouldn't disappear overnight if the New York press would just go out of business. But it's the *Republic* we want to hear about on that shoddy Los Angeles porch with the bile-colored sunset, and the fear of the dark, and half a carton of milk in the icebox. We want to hear someone speak with love and faith of the Republic—someone who knows, who bears the responsibility.

And we don't. And it's strange that we don't, for the Republic is still here, is still constantly referred to as the richest country in the world, the most powerful in history. If ever a political experiment could be said to have succeeded, ours can be said to have succeeded. Twice in its history the Republic has had to adjust itself to catastrophe and twice it has gone on, stronger, more sure of itself, more certain. It survived the bloodiest civil war in human history and, seventy years later, recovered from the almost total collapse of its economic system—recovered, what's more, with its fundamental law and its underlying conception of itself intact. No political idea which can change to meet the changes of time, adapt itself to the disasters of history, and still be true to the hope which defined it can be written off as a failure no matter what new evils threaten.

Why then this frightened generation? If men in the generation before the Civil War, when the great experiment seemed really doomed, could feel about the Union as John Quincy Adams did and Emerson and Clay—even Calhoun—if men in Webster's time could love the country with all its faults upon it, trust it with all its faults, why cannot we? We of all Americans? For *we* are the generation which faced the horror of the anti-experiment—the fascism of Hitler and Stalin. We know, as men before us never knew, what the opposite of freedom can be. Why have *we* not remembered?

I suppose to ask that question is to answer it: no one who lived through the Second World War and the Stalin terror could ever forget what the opposite of freedom is, but freedom itself, the great positive dream of freedom, is a different matter. A man or a nation needs help to see that vision. It is its writers who make a country visible to itself. Shakespeare created England for the English—Shakespeare and Chaucer and the rest. Tolstoy and Turgenev and Dostoevski created Russia in the Russian mind, and it is the tragedy of Russia today that the one man capable of recreating the nation

3

after the delirium of the Stalin years has been silenced by an ignorant bureaucracy—a tragedy not only for the Communist bureaucracy and for Solzhenitsyn and for Russia but for the world. But what then of ourselves? We too had ministers of light: Whitman and Emerson and Melville and Mark Twain. We learned the Republic from their words and from Lincoln's. Where are they now or their successors? The latest serious attempt by an able novelist to show us what and who we are was Dos Passos's *U.S.A.*, but the America of *U.S.A.* was the America of the Thirties, and since that time American writers have left the great theme of the common life to the sociologists, who have done their best with their polls and statistics—bricks without straw—but have not given us what we need to know.

But is this truly the cause of our loss of heart? —that we do not love the Republic as we once did because we do not know it as we once did? And that we do not know it as we once did because there is no voice to tell? Because Whitman's long halloo comes now from too far away? Because Melville's words are drowned in a wind from the sea and the sea is now foreign to us? Because Faulkner wrote of a country of his own and the roads in that country now are strange, the roofs distant. Because later, lesser novelists took to city streets and bedroom closets, rediscovering, not the Republic, but the thoughts of Sigmund Freud? Well, it's always pleasant to put the blame on somebody else—particularly writers—but when it comes to a trouble like ours, a cloud of troubles, the vicarious responsibility doesn't work. Whitman can conceive a believable America, but when you yourself no longer believe in it the responsibility has to be yours because the doubt is yours—because the fear is yours. If you find, searching your heart, that you no longer love your country as older and possibly wiser Americans loved it, the reason cannot be in them. Where then will you turn to find it?

Most of us would have an easy answer: you turn to the country. It is the country which has changed, not we. But *has* the country changed, or is it the time which has changed? The age? The epoch? The epoch everywhere and in every country? The world crisis in which we live—population crisis, pollution crisis, weapon crisis, race crisis, human crisis? Taken together, as they must be taken, they make a grim bag— the grimmest perhaps in the whole experience of mankind. But because the times are bad does it follow that the *Republic* made them bad? That the *American Proposition* is to blame? That all would be well if it were not for those Self-Evident Truths in which we put our trust—those unalienable rights established by the Declaration of Independence and the first ten amendments to the Constitution?

There is opinion to the right of us as well as opinion to the left which makes precisely that argument, though not in just those words. The Tories of the Old Right have never accepted the Declaration of Independence except on the Fourth of July: to assert that "all men" have unalienable rights is to extend those rights to men accused of crimes and thus, as the Tories say, to tie the hands of the police. And as for the Left, there are students —even intelligent students from good universities— who go so far as to contend that the great American past is to blame for the worst aspects of the American present—the ravaged continent and the polluted air. If it had not been for the American Revolution, they say, and the great Declaration and the Bill of Rights there would have been no nonsense about individual freedom, and if there had been no individual freedom there would have been no rugged individualism, and if there had been no rugged individualism the Merrimack River would still flow clean and clear as it did when Thoreau paddled on it. From which it follows, as from dark the day, that the only effective cure for Lake Erie is to junk the Republic and start all over with the Thoughts of Chairman Mao. Which is a little extreme but not as startling as the fact, presented in testimony before Senator Sam Ervin's subcommittee, that when a copy of the Bill of Rights was presented to casual passers-by on the streets of Madison, Wisconsin, one of the most enlightened towns in the Middle West, 111 persons refused to approve the principles set forth in the document as compared with one who agreed to sign. What would happen if a similar experiment were attempted in Washington no one knows, but it has been frequently stated and is widely believed that if the Bill of Rights were now introduced into the Congress as new legislation it would be overwhelmingly defeated in the House.

So there are those—and not only radical students and Right-wing politicians—who believe that the American Idea, the American Proposition, is in some way to blame for the miseries we live among. The news would startle even Benjamin Franklin, who was rarely startled by anything. And it ought, I think, to startle us. It is only human nature, perhaps, to look for scapegoats when an age goes bad, but this particular attribution of blame is too irrational even for human nature. Not because blame is levelled against the Republic. There are many things for which we ought to bear the responsibility and do—as, for example, the Asian War. But because we bear that responsibility it does not follow that the state of the ravaged earth should be charged to our account and, above all, to the account of our principles, our beliefs. The crisis of our age is not an American crisis no matter what the ignorant and the immature may say. Metropolitan crowding, unburied refuse, flowing filth may be more visible in the United States than elsewhere because the processes which produce these things were carried farther in the United States than in other countries, but reeking air and blackened cities existed under the Hanoverian kings and the Holy Alliance long before they turned up in Massachusetts and Pennsylvania, and rivers run as nasty black in a Marxist state as in a free society.

No, these are worldwide consequences because their cause is a world cause: the Industrial Revolution . . . or, more precisely, the counter-revolution in the ecology which the Industrial Revolution has precipitated. For 200 years we in the West had thought of the Industrial Revolution as another name for progress: warmer, if not more

beautiful, housing; better and more abundant food; cheaper clothing; longer lives—a whole roster of comforts and conveniences and even luxuries never before conceived. And now suddenly in a matter of years, months almost, we find ourselves presented with a vast, worldwide accounting for all this: a balance sheet almost entirely in the red which tots up costs we never thought of in the old enthusiastic days when rivers which provided drinking water and cheap transportation were made to serve as sewers also and a multiplying population was a sign, not of imminent disaster, but of an endlessly expanding prosperity.

But though this sad accounting is presented in every industrialized country on earth—in Japan and China as in England and France, in Chile as in the United States—the curious notion still persists in this country that we Americans are principally responsible and that our responsibility involves the freedom of our society, the institutions which made us free. Just as the word "Americanize" was used a generation ago to describe the worst changes made by industrialization in Europe, so the same word is used today to define the worst *consequences* of industrialization everywhere. And used not only by Europeans and Africans and Asiatics but by ourselves. The young, generous in their indignation as the young so often are, accept a guilt for their country which history will certainly not assign, and the result is a noticeable increase in the almost morbid self-reproach which now afflicts Americans, shaking their faith in their country, in their history, and in themselves.

It is not a healthy situation. A decent humility is an admirable thing in any society, but a morbid self-abnegation is not—particularly when it undermines the confidence of a free people in their freedom, in the laws and institutions which defend their freedom. What we need to do in the United States is to take a long, hard look at ourselves *as a people*. Specifically, what we need to do is to look at the facts, not the fears, and to distinguish ourselves as human beings from ourselves as statistical victims of the population crisis, the pollution crisis, the earth crisis. Our dilemma is that of all mankind, but our institutions and our history are our own, and our ability to act effectively in the crisis of our time will depend on our institutions, on our history. We need to remind ourselves of that fact, to get our guilt in perspective, to remember our past and our pride and to ask ourselves with a cold eye whether we believe *in truth* what we hear ourselves saying we believe—what we hear our politicians saying for us.

This book does not address itself explicitly to questions such as these but it asks them. It invites our attention once again to images of the continent, of the Republic, of the people who are the Republic. And by these images it suggests, without argument or pleading, that we reconsider what we really think. We tell each other often enough that the country has gone to Hell, but has it? Do we really think it has? We listen to politicians who tell us that nothing can save the Republic but the FBI and the Pentagon and that even they will be helpless unless we surrender a bit of our freedom—let Big Brother bug our telephone conversations. Though we listen to talk like that, do we really believe it? We vote for demagogues who tell us in double talk, in secret signals, that the great American Proposition that all men are created equal is nonsense. But do we really vote against that Proposition? And is it *these* men we mean—the men and women whose images face us on these pages?

You can't photograph a proposition. You can't even photograph equality. Some men are taller than others, some are stronger than others, abler, healthier. And yet the proposition and the equality are in these images. Look at them. Look at the faces. What do you see? Self-respect, first and foremost: sometimes belligerent self-respect, more often something stronger and quieter. And what is *self*-respect? When it is real, as it is here, it is respect for what you share with others and what they share with you—respect for common humanity. But if that is so, what then is the *equal* thing? The human-

ity. A man who believes the American Proposition that all men are created equal is a man who believes that all men are human and must be respected accordingly—all men including himself—himself and therefore all men. But is this nonsense? When you vote for your demagogue, are you telling the world you think all this is nonsense?

And there are other questions about these faces you see here. They believe in their equality whether you do or not, but there is something else they believe in. They believe in what goes *with* the equality. They believe that a free people is free to bear responsibilities as well as to enjoy freedom, and this is a rare thing in the world. Most of the peoples of the world, and increasingly as the police states proliferate, regard it as no part of their duty to concern themselves with the common life. You look out for yourself and leave all the rest to the Party or the bureaucracy or the church or the government or the army or whatever. We in America began with a different notion: the best government, so far as we were concerned, was the least government. Which meant that we staked out a margin of the common life for ourselves—education, religion, health, and the like. We claimed the ground and we accepted the responsibility. The first settlers established the principle and later settlers adopted it, regardless of their experience in the old country. And by the time we were halfway through our history we had become a people wholly unlike any other in our theory and practice of the management of the business of living. We did for ourselves what most peoples left to the authorities. It was the *people* who put up the first schools in the country, and the earliest (and still the best) of our colleges and universities were their work—as were (and are) the great hospitals and the first social services.

Furthermore, that sense of responsibility has survived into the time of the welfare state and has grown, developed. New generations of Americans have accepted responsibilities not only in the old marginal area but even, when government failed to act, on the government ground itself. Nothing could be more clearly the duty of government under the American system than the protection of the civil rights guaranteed by the Constitution, and for no category of civil rights had the government a more obvious responsibility than for the rights of the descendants of those who had been abducted and enslaved and whom the Republic, warring against itself, had fought to free. But, when Congress after Congress failed to act, the people—and not the blacks alone but whites also, young and old, women as well as men—forced the issue and compelled the federal government to accept its Constitutional obligation. Nor did the Civil Rights Movement of the Sixties exhaust the impulse of the American people to do for themselves what a corrupt or impotent Congress failed to do for them. In the agony of the cities, in the revolt of the consumers against the vast conglomerates which have exploited them, it is the citizen-sense which provides a foothold for action.

And nowhere else is that uniquely American resource more hopeful than precisely in the ecological crisis which has driven some to despair of our future. The ecological crisis has existed throughout the world for many years, but where did it first become a great public issue? In the Peoples' Republics so-called?—the great police states of Europe and Asia? Certainly not. Industry in a People's Republic is a state monopoly, and no one challenges a state monopoly in a country where the police walk in without knocking. Where then? Precisely in the United States, in the homeland of the vast corporations, and against their protests.

And why did it happen here? Because the American people had accepted for themselves and thereby asserted for themselves the ultimate responsibility of management (it was *their* continent) and because American industry, with all its monopolistic tendencies and exploitative urge, had been oriented from the beginning toward the people's

demands. Ours was a consumer society—meaning, not as it sometimes does today, a society existing for the purpose of consumption, but a society existing for the satisfaction of human needs, a society which created, with the products demanded by those needs, the means of acquiring them. Henry Ford's assembly lines, like Eli Whitney's use of interchangeable parts, were economic as well as industrial innovations. They multiplied products to bring prices within reach and they raised wages, turning laborers into customers, until, as this book remarks, the Republic was able to share "larger amounts of goods among more people than any other nation in human history." Not all the consequences, of course, were happy. American materialism was one—"the affluent society." But the fundamental achievement nothing can change. A successful society had been created, the overriding purpose of which was to provide for human life—not only for the survival of human life but for its enlargement, its enfranchisement. The great conception of the American premise, which it is fashionable now to deride as a splurge of Eighteenth Century rhetoric, had imposed itself on the new technology to create the possibility of a practical human freedom. And if the new technology brought with it the crisis that we, like all the rest of humanity must now face, it brought too the human means of confronting it.

The time is ripe, or so it would seem to me, for a reconsideration, not of our ancestors' ideas about our country but of our own: not what they *thought* but what we think we think. Their ideas have lasted 200 years and have proved themselves sounder with each new challenge. Ours—our fears on the Right, our rhetoric on the Left—are feebler with every repetition. Try them against the images in this book: the continent, the endless sky, the *human faces*.

*The flag still flies on quiet, sun-drenched streets in
our country, and the Fourth of July is still a time for parades.
The flag is still a trusted symbol of hope in our country.
And when it goes by little boys still stand—straight and
proud and tall—with their fathers. In our country!*

This is a book about America.
It is a testament of faith—faith in our people,
our values and our institutions—published at
a time when it appears to be more fashionable
to criticize what's wrong with America than
to affirm what is right, or can be made right, in America.

There is history in these pages because we cannot know
who we are or where we are going without understanding
something about our heritage, where we came from, what we
have achieved. But this is not a history book. Its emphasis,
in both text and pictures, is on our country as it is today.

Most of the photographs on these pages were taken
within the last two or three years. There are vistas of the
beautiful land and of the things that we have built upon it.
There are closeups of people at work and at play—young
people and old people, rich people and just plain people,
black people and white and red and yellow people,
artists and scientists, doers and dreamers.

To look at these photographs is to see ourselves as
we are and as we have been shaped by this, our country.

Land of Opportunity

Lumahai Beach, Kauai, Hawaii

Nubble Light, Maine

Druid Arch, Canyonlands National Park, Utah

Lake Ann, Cascade Range, Washington

Mendenhall Glacier, Alaska

Great Sand Dunes National Monument, Colorado

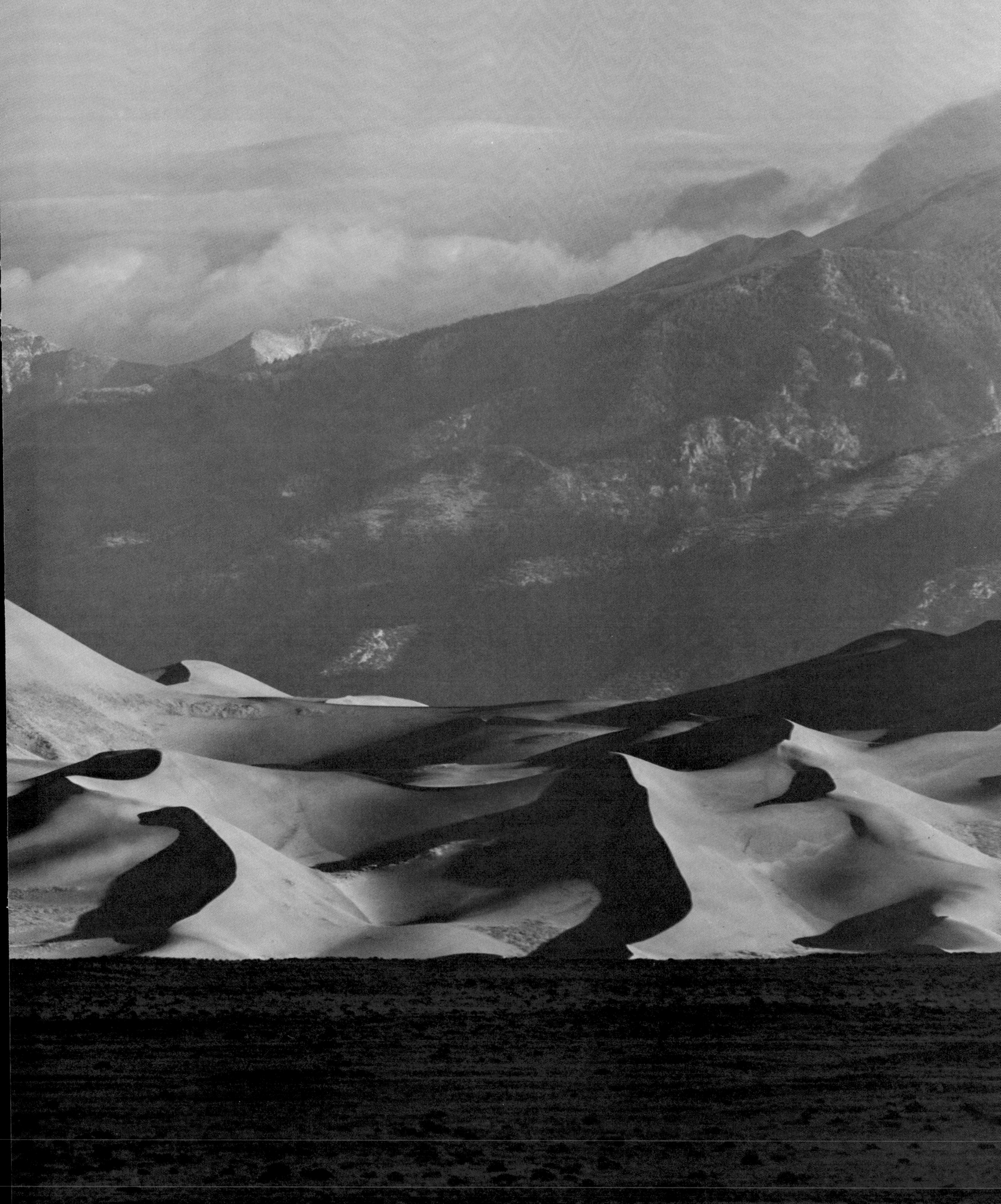

Country road south of Arlington, Vermont

St. Nicholas, Minnesota

Contoured farmland southwest of Millersville, Pennsylvania

Rocky Mountains, Colorado

Skykomish River and the Wenatchee mountains in Washington

Cactus in Saguaro
National Monument, Arizona

Near Tucson, Arizona, the 18th century
mission church of San Xavier del Bac

Goblin Valley, Utah

South rim of the Grand Canyon, Arizona

The will to explore, the freedom to experiment

The land has always been beautiful. Seamen from Europe glimpsed first the Atlantic breaking on long, white beaches; behind the sands, birds rose in clouds from the marshes, and the forests of the coastal plain marched down to the water's edge. Rivers led on through pine and oak enough for all the navies of a sailing world, past cliffs and hills, outposts of the blue mountains that fringed the shore. One river—the Hudson—broke through the Appalachians and opened a way toward the mighty lakes, toward those other rivers—the Ohio, the Mississippi, the Missouri—that drained the great, fertile center of the continent.

And beyond the Mississippi, up the muddy Missouri, lay the plains, vast in extent, sloping upward to the Rocky Mountains; down to the dry lands, dusted faint green with paloverde, studded with monstrous shapes of old eroded hills and carved into deep canyons. The tall Sierra Nevadas loomed still farther west, across the deserts: mountains of stark form and color, tipped with snow, traversed by high, difficult passes leading into the California valleys and to the Coast Range that dipped so briskly to the Pacific Ocean.

The richness of the land was only hinted at in the beginning by dense forest growth and green, flower-spangled meadows and prairies; by numberless streams, alive with fish, where the beaver wrought endlessly; by ranging moose and herds of deer in the woodlands; by the elk, wild goat, and sheep which roamed the mountains; by black hordes of bison and scampering antelope on the plains.

This was not the ready-made wealth of a Golconda or of Montezuma or the Incas, to freight a galleon and enrich a plunderer. This was

Aspen trees
in the Rockies

land to be tilled, with hard labor and persistent courage. But above all it was a plastic land, open beyond the dreams of those who came from close-built Europe, a land where institutions could be shaped along new lines; where change was not only possible but constantly required; where the wealth that was wrung from the soil could be shared in ways different from those of older societies; and where man's adaptation to his environment and to his fellows was not prescribed by ancient precedents or enforced by hereditary authority. It was the "otherwise minded" who came to live in this land, those who marched—and still march—to a different drum. They were restless and unafraid, and they marched across—and eventually settled—an entire continent.

So it is that when the sun now rises out of the Atlantic, it lights up a landscape vastly transformed since Verrazano coasted its shores or Hudson probed its rivers; since the Pilgrims landed at Plymouth or Ponce de Leon sought the fountain of youth in Florida.

In approximately four centuries, the beautiful land has become the home of nearly 210 million people whose ancestry includes every race on earth. Their ships are in the harbors; their trains and automobiles span the continent; their planes criss-cross the skies. And their homes are everywhere: along rocky shores in Maine and white beaches in Florida, on wheat farms in the Middle West and in the citrus groves of California, bordering the tundra in Alaska and under tropic palms in Hawaii. The very sun takes eight hours to speed across this land, with its fifty states spread from Penobscot Bay to Honolulu, and from Attu to Key West.

The transformation of the land, physically and in terms of human habitability, was one of the major events in human history—comparable to the folk-wanderings that settled Europe and unsettled the Roman Empire, to the vast movements of the Bantu-speaking peoples that, more recently, changed the face of Africa. The pioneers who traversed, settled, and developed this land had something to work with—fertile soil, a favorable climate, and vast resources in minerals and timber. But, as the late industrialist, S. Bayard Colgate, once told the Committee for Economic Development, "at the time our Constitution was drawn up other countries had equally fertile soil, other countries had more abundant labor, larger amounts of capital, better educational institutions, better roads and other means of communication, and natural resources more adequate for the agrarian economies of those times."

What we had in greater measure was the will to try new things, to adopt new values, to experiment—to accept change rather than to resist it. "Change and attempted improvements," according to the Committee for Economic Development, "have been in the very genes of the millions of immigrants who have come to our land over the centuries.

Mount Whitney in the Sierra Nevada Mountains of California

Many came seeking freedom in a very wide sense—freedom from government domination; freedom from church domination; freedom from class rigidity. An urge toward 'progress' has been part and parcel of our thinking, of our social environment, from the days of the earliest settlers. Our people, no matter whence they came, tended quickly to throw off the old and seek the new." And ours has always been a form of government which provided *freedom* to change, which not only permitted but even encouraged change.

Election day in November produces another phenomenon, one that does much to explain the nature of the society that transformed the land, developed a continent, and forged that special entity known as the United States of America.

On that day, millions of Americans go to the polls to decide who shall be their chief magistrate. (In 1968, the son of a grocer defeated a former pharmacist in the campaign for this high office). They assemble in many places to vote: in stores and churches, schools and apartment house lobbies, in person or by mail, using paper ballots or machines. At some polling places there are long lines; at others only a few queue up for the privilege. In Delaware, a voting machine and three election officials may again be trucked to Bread and Cheese Island, to permit Eugene and May Sheats, who were the only voters in that tiny district in 1968, to exercise the supreme right of American citizenship.

For the whole thrust of this mass action is to give free expression to the will of the people in determining who will be their leaders and how the government of the country is to be run. Not only are a President and Vice President to be selected; one-third of the Senate and the whole House of Representatives go before the electorate. Many state governors and legislators, judges, mayors, city councilmen, and county selectmen—along with other candidates for office, national, state, and local—present themselves to the citizenry and ask for their votes.

Issues as well as men who represent issues, regulations for and against the serving of alcoholic beverages, laws to fix new voting districts and clear old slums, ordinances regulating the heights of buildings—these and many other options are contested all over the country.

In 1968, the campaign was a tempestuous one, with controversies over the war in Vietnam raging across the nation. President Lyndon Johnson decided not to seek a second term, largely because of those controversies. A principal Democratic contender, Senator Robert Kennedy, was murdered, as his brother, President John F. Kennedy, had been before him. There were those who felt that the major parties did not present a clear-cut choice to the nation. Rioting in the streets marred the sessions of the Democratic National Convention in Chicago, and there

Republican National Convention in Miami, 1968

Democratic National
Convention in
Chicago, 1968

were more riots on election day in several cities across the country.

But—and this is significant—no riots were directed against the election process itself, and none seriously affected it. And although Richard Nixon was elected by a very slender plurality, almost as slender as that by which he had been defeated in 1960, the transition from Democratic to Republican leadership of the nation was smooth and orderly—just as it had been when the Democrat Kennedy succeeded the Republican Eisenhower; just as it had been when Vice President Johnson took over from the dead hand of Kennedy; just as had always been the case (with the tragic exception of the secession and civil war that followed Abraham Lincoln's election in 1860) throughout the history of the United States. The beautiful land has a free government that works.

It is a government that expresses one of the primary principles of the American experience, that of the voluntary society. The election of a President, after his selection as a candidate by one of the major parties, is only the culmination of a process with many facets. Even his power, when elected, can be affected by innumerable votes for other purposes and other causes, down to the smallest local subdivision, down to the most hopeless independent candidacy.

National elections demonstrate again and again how the voluntary principle operates—how, even in a nation of 210 million, there can be participatory democracy for those who are really willing to participate. Obviously, it is a complex operation, one in which a vote on a local bond issue or a door-bell-ringing campaign for a maverick candidate has its place, no less than a vote for the President of the United States. It is a process indigenous to America. And it began when groups and individuals found their way to these shores and set about governing themselves.

When the first white settlers camped along the fringes of what is now the United States of America and sent adventurous wanderers into the interior, they found others who had come before them. Perhaps four million, possibly more than five million, Indians and Eskimos already lived between the Rio Grande and the extreme limits of habitability in the Arctic. Immigrants themselves, over millenia, from Asia, they had evolved scores of widely different societies to meet the challenge of their environment. In the Northwest, the Indians decorated their plank houses with carvings and lived fatly on salmon and halibut; in the Mohawk Valley, there were whole towns surrounded by palisades and tilled fields. From the economically stark and culturally simple life of the Shoshone to the elaborate social structure of the Natchez there was a wide range of patterns for living, of values that are only now, perhaps, gaining belated recognition among those who cherish the diversity of our culture.

For these values were so different from those exported from Eu-

Kennedy and Eisenhower leave for the Capitol, January 20, 1961.

Inauguration of President Nixon, January 20, 1969

rope in a day when historical perspective was minimal and tolerance of alien ideas was in its infancy that they had little impact upon the white society growing up along the shores and on the riverbanks. More, the Indians were thinly scattered, their economies required large areas for support, and their own political structures were fitted mostly to small groups. The Iroquois confederation was unusual; alliances of tribes tended to be short-lived. And the Indians were easy prey to illnesses to which Europeans had built up at least partial immunity; the tragedy of the Polynesians in the South Seas was prefigured in America.

Thus, the beautiful land was not empty when the newcomers came from across the Atlantic, but had many blank spaces on which they could make their own mark.

Some of the Europeans simply brought the ideas of an older world to the new. They wished to recreate British manors, French seigneuries, Dutch patroonships or Spanish haciendas. Or, in a spirit that was newly abroad in the seventeenth century, they formed companies to extract the new land's wealth by any means that seemed possible—fur-trading or fishing, lumbering or farming.

But within and without these essentially exploitative thrusts was something else—the dream of a better life than had been known before. This dream was usually a highly personal one, a matter of individual conscience or aspiration. And so it gave one characteristic to the people who were to settle this land: individualism.

But since man cannot create a society of single separate cells, individuals came together in free association to work out common means for defense, for organizing a community, for governing it. When the Mayflower lay at anchor off Plymouth in the chill November of 1620, the Separatists—the Pilgrim Fathers themselves—and other men in the group that had been dispatched under the auspices of the company of London merchants who financed the expedition, affixed their names to a compact. Stating their allegiance to "our dread soveraigne Lord" King James I, the intending colonists affirmed that they were establishing a "body politick," to "enacte, constitute, and frame such just & equal Lawes, ordinances, Acts, constitutions, & offices, from time to time, as shall be thought most meete & convenient for ye generall good of ye colonie, unto which we promise all due submission and obedience."

John Quincy Adams has called this document—the Mayflower Compact—"the first example in modern times of a social compact or system of government instituted by voluntary agreement, conformable to the laws of nature, by men of equal rights, and about to establish their community in a new country."

Certainly the compact was a succinct expression of that spirit of

voluntarism which was to run like a sustaining stream through American history. The Separatists had followed their consciences out of the Church of England and, by way of Leyden in the Netherlands, to the New World. They had agreed together, without distinctions of class or sect, to make their own laws—and to obey them.

Other colonies, of other men and women, from other lands, were already fixed in America. When the Mayflower reached Plymouth, there were already Englishmen in Virginia, indentured servants had already acquired land, a representative assembly had already been held. Spaniards had established permanent settlements in Florida, Frenchmen were fanning out through the West. Before the end of the seventeenth century, the Dutch were on the Hudson, Swedes were in Delaware, Germans were migrating to Pennsylvania. The French (except for some Huguenots) were Catholic, so were the Spanish. English Catholics, too, settled in Maryland, as Anglicans had done in Virginia; there were Congregationalists in New England, Mennonites and Friends in Pennsylvania; Baptists and other denominations found refuge in Rhode Island, and Jews came there and to New York where the Dutch had their Reformed Church. In the Carolinas, Scotch, English, and French colonists cleared land and built their homes.

The immigrants came for many reasons, but most came with a conviction that some special Providence—whatever name, cult or philosophy might be given to it—rested upon the land, and on them as dwellers in it. And out of their experience in this New World, no less than from the lessons and the thinking of the Old, they distilled a practical dream.

They had brought with them many of the social, religious, and political preconceptions of their varied homelands. But, remote from the stratifications of the older nations, the colonial American had also to test new methods of government, based on the facts of his egalitarian existence, rather than on the written precedents of history.

As the eighteenth century British statesman, Edmund Burke, said of this process: "Through a wise and salutary neglect, a generous nature has been suffered to take her own way to perfection." And the result found magnificent expression in the Declaration of Independence:

"We hold these truths to be self-evident, that all men are created equal, that they are endowed by their Creator with certain unalienable Rights, that among these are Life, Liberty, and the Pursuit of Happiness. That to secure these rights, Governments are instituted among Men, deriving their just Powers from the Consent of the Governed,—That whenever any Form of Government becomes destructive of these ends, it is the Right of the People to alter or to abolish it, and to institute new Government, laying its foundation on such principles, and organizing its

35

powers in such form, as to them shall seem most likely to affect their Safety and Happiness."

These words were momentous precisely because the truths that were self-evident to the Continental Congress and the armies that fought under Washington were far from being recognized by a world in which the equality of mankind before the law was expressly denied by virtually every human society; in which government was the God-given right of dynasties and castes; in which rebellion was far more than a civil crime—it was a moral and religious sin.

Now the truths of the Declaration are so self-evident that hardly a government around the globe does not pay them at least lip service; the most radical of America's questing youth does not challenge them, but rather the institutions that have been set up in their name. But all the familiarity, all the dispute over their precise application, and all the widespread acceptance should not be allowed to obscure the fact that in their day, and for many years thereafter, those truths were new. Their enunciation and the measures taken to put them into effect—even the tragic Civil War, its causes so closely entwined with differing interpretations of the Declaration and the Constitution—mingled with the beauty and the riches of the land to form a great magnet for the peoples of the world.

George Washington said of the Constitution: "Let us raise a standard to which the wise and honest can repair." No one could claim that it was only the wise and the honest who crowded the decks of sailing ships, the steerages of steamers or the passenger lists of jetliners. But down through the years, more people came from more different places to form the United States of America than in any mass migration in history.

In the words of Archibald MacLeish: "They were the first self-constituted, self-declared, self-created People in the history of the world."

The great majority came from Europe—an estimated 30 million persons before 1914. In the beginning, most were from northwestern Europe; in the last half of the nineteenth and early part of the twentieth centuries they poured in from eastern, central, and southern Europe as well. Together, these tides washed into the Atlantic ports and then moved westward at varying rates of speed.

The earlier migrants marched on ahead—with an advance guard of trappers, woods runners, and plainsmen to break trail—in search of cheaper, richer land, and of the opportunities developing communities proffered. For the first generation immigrants did not, as a general thing, take up land on the frontier or elsewhere. In 1870, for example, only 10 percent of foreign-born Americans were farmers—although the great majority had been peasants in Europe, displaced or unhappy because of the

37

problems inherent in the industrial revolution and in agricultural tenures in the lands of their birth.

Most of these, as historian Oscar Handlin points out, had neither the capital nor the incentives immediately to purchase land, build homes, and buy farm equipment. In European terms, the land was extremely low in cost—$2.50, $1.25, or, after the Homestead Act of 1862, actually nothing an acre, out of a public domain of more than two billion acres—and houses might be built of logs in wooded areas, and of sod on the prairies. But most of the immigrants found it easier to join the pool of unskilled labor that a new, rich country in the springtime of the industrial revolution needed to dig its canals, lay ties, and cut roadbeds for its railways, work the mines and forests, and feed the foundries and factories that were springing up across the land.

Initially, for the most part, the immigrants clotted in the port cities where they landed, unused to city ways and lacking urban skills. The slums they lived in were the first stop for an uprooted rural people not yet qualified for any but the lowest rung on the urban ladder. It took a generation, sometimes more, for succeeding waves of immigrants to develop the skills they needed to establish themselves economically and socially in this land of opportunity. But gradually, most of the Irish, the Italians, and the Jews of eastern Europe moved out of the crowded inner cities. Now, with greater restrictions on immigration, it is the unskilled and displaced of America—many of them black—who are finding their way to the cities, beginning that process that so many ethnic groups had undertaken before them.

Not that immigration has ended, or that the beautiful land has lost its hold on the imagination of the world. Far from it. In spite of the restrictions which have been placed on immigration, nearly 400,000 new immigrants still enter every year, and many more would undoubtedly do so if permitted by their own and the American authorities.

One group of new immigrants—the 700,000 Cubans who have come here since Fidel Castro attained power in January of 1959—has proved once again that the United States is a haven for the persecuted and the afflicted. The New York harbor of the earlier immigrants, for these Cubans, has been Miami's bustling airport. Most are destitute on arrival as were those who came more than a century ago, but approximately 60 percent of the Cubans living in or near Miami already own or are buying their own homes, and there are about 6,000 Cuban-owned businesses in the area. Miami has now become a bilingual city. About half the Cuban immigrants have moved out of Florida and have set up new homes in all of the other 49 states. Some 80 percent of all Cubans in the United States are now self-supporting, with an average annual

Cuban refugee doctor,
architect (above), bank president (left)
and drugstore owner (below)

family income of more than $6,000.

This twentieth century success story follows the older patterns of immigration, but has been speeded up by what one official called the "pure guts" of the refugees. To be sure, they are an elite group, with high ratios of professional, managerial, and technical skills. But, as with older groups of immigrants, it took guts to leave accustomed surroundings and to start with nothing in a strange land, among people of different speech and customs. Also like the immigrants of an earlier time, the Cubans are individualists—people who would not conform to the dictates of a Castro or a Guevara. But when they came here they quickly formed associations to help each other, and were helped by voluntary associations of Americans anxious to assist the strangers to find their way. Clubs and churches, commercial and cultural associations have always marked the entry of ethnic groups into America, just as such associations marched with the pioneers across the plains and mountains.

On the frontier, such associations were indispensable. They might be as comprehensive and enduring as the organization the Church of Jesus Christ of the Latter-Day Saints (the Mormons) took to Utah, or they might be as occasional as a cattle roundup, a barn-raising, or a husking bee. The pioneers gathered together to form wagon trains beyond the wide Missouri, to organize defenses against Indians and outlaws, to build a school or lobby for a railway. And wherever they went, from Plymouth Rock in Massachusetts to Seal Rocks in California, they brought this habit of association with them.

Nearly a century and a half ago, de Tocqueville, the French statesman and political scientist who wrote the most penetrating and enduring analysis of the American and his particular institutions, stated that: "In no country in the world has the principal of association been more successfully used, or applied to a greater multitude of objects than America." And Hannah Arendt, the writer and educator whose insights and understanding supplement those of de Tocqueville, asserts that this phrase is equally true today.

Out of individualism, then, and free association, Americans have created a voluntary society with greater freedom of expression and action than any other nation of comparable size in the world. Whether it derived directly from the frontier experience, or from a selective use of Old World institutions and ideas—or a combination of these—is a question that has exercised historians. Nor can this be considered merely an academic matter. For if American democracy is primarily a product of the frontier, as historian Frederick Jackson Turner and many others have alleged, what would happen when the frontier disappeared, when it was no longer out west somewhere to test the mettle of impatient dissenters and the adventurous young? By 1901, the last major Indian uprising had been quelled at Wounded Knee Creek, the last major area of the public domain had been opened to settlement in Oklahoma, and most of the good free land had been occupied. The frontier, if Alaska is excluded, had virtually vanished.

"Slowly we shall grow old," wrote Woodrow Wilson in 1893, "compact our people, study the delicate adjustments of an intricate society, and ponder the niceties, as we have hitherto pondered the bulks and structural framework of government."

In some ways, this may be an accurate portrayal of America today. But if the United States is maturing, it is not yet aged. When one considers the creative experimentation and action with which this country met the great depression of the 1930s, the gigantic effort of the 1940s (even more impressive industrially and in terms of mass popular effort than in a strictly military sense), the economic development following World War II, and the striving and searching to improve the quality of life that marked the 1960s, there is no evidence of the hardening of the nation's arteries which Wilson seemed to anticipate.

Rather, each of these stages, over the past forty years, has revealed the same restless quest for new answers, the same refusal to accept what is in place of what might be. Americans have long since reached the Pacific and moved on to Hawaii and Alaska. We have even reached the moon. But the challenge of the 1970s, for those with the vision and the courage to break new ground, is neither "out west" nor in outer space. It is right here at home, in the social and economic problems that face this nation— and every other developed nation in the world.

Those problems are large. Not every American is by choice or inheritance a member of the voluntary society. There are the Indians, perhaps 800,000 in number, divorced from their cultural roots, surrounded by an alien society which has neither absorbed them nor permitted them to live the free lives their ancestors knew. There are the blacks—11 percent of the total population—most descendants of slaves, forcibly transported to the beautiful land and, though free by law, too often penned in by poverty and prejudice. There are those with Spanish-speaking backgrounds—said now to include 5 percent of all Americans. The Cubans have come of their own volition to escape Communist repression. The Puerto Ricans were brought under the American flag in 1898 as a result of the Spanish-American War, and—in a 1967 referendum—overwhelmingly voted to remain in special Commonwealth status. Those who come to the continental United States do so by choice, and they have full voting and civil rights. As for the Chicanos—the Mexican-Americans—many are descended from those who lived in territories ac-

Dr. Martin Luther King delivers "I have a dream" speech at Lincoln Memorial August 28, 1963.

Dr. King leads Selma-to-Montgomery civil rights marchers, March 21, 1965.

40

Mrs. Rosa Parks, who started the
Montgomery, Alabama, bus boycott in 1955

quired in the war with Mexico, many others came in as migrants.

Each of these groups poses a challenge to the American capacity for equitable absorption. As primarily a rural people seeking new lives in the cities, they also face the age-old problem of adaptation, and on a scale that helps make America's urban question perhaps its most vital one. Even transportation—to the extent that urban centers and their ties to one another and to the suburbs are at the heart of the difficulty—is linked to these other issues, as is the matter of air and water pollution.

But more fundamental than even these serious problems is the unease so many Americans, of all classes and colors, feel in the very massiveness of the complex society in which they dwell. They fear a poverty of spirit, a sense of being mere cogs in an agglomeration of wheels. In many ways, the passing of the old frontier and the very ease of modern transportation in our affluent society are leaving their marks. The earlier American, when afflicted by the "November of the soul" that troubled Herman Melville's Ishmael, would go to sea or take to the woods. Now our waterways are jammed with pleasure boats, and even 200 million or more acres of national and state parks do not seem to be enough to accommodate the cars and trailers of vacationing families.

But even when the solitude of wild lands and open seas beckoned, the American has always felt some of this recurring discontent. As long ago as 1841, Lord Carlisle wrote that the United States "was probably the country in which there was less misery and less happiness than in any other of the world."

People from less favored lands find it difficult to understand this phenomenon. A recently naturalized American, six years away from Poland, addressed herself to her fellow Americans through the free press: "Among some of our American-born friends it is not fashionable to be enthusiastic about America. There is Vietnam, drugs, urban and racial conflicts, poverty and pollution. Undoubtedly, this country faces urgent and serious problems. But what we, the newcomers, see are not only the problems but also democratic solutions being sought and applied." For Janina Atkins and her husband, America was not a land overflowing with milk and honey. But they were delighted to be able to buy a needle at Woolworth's, and not to have to pay a day's earnings for a small chicken. They could vote as free citizens of a free country—there was "no one here to lead you by the hand, but also no one to order you about."

There is no doubt, today, that democratic solutions are still being sought and applied, and in them is the adventure of the spirit that America provides. Mrs. Rosa Parks, one December day in 1955, refused to move to the back of a Montgomery, Alabama, bus. As a black, she was arrested. Martin Luther King, Jr., took up her cause and that of his race.

41

There was a boycott of the bus line, blacks organized, and eventually the Supreme Court of the United States ruled that segregation by race in public accommodations violates the Constitution.

This was a beginning in that great stirring which is moving the American people to correct old ills and live up to old ideals, to make the Constitution conform to the Declaration of Independence by the means foreshadowed in the Mayflower Compact. One individual can start such a stirring, another may inspire it, but many—working together in voluntary association—can bring it to fruition.

So in 1970 we had federal watchers at the polls, to insure that each voter's rights were respected. We now have black mayors in Newark, New Jersey, in Gary, Indiana, and in other cities. When one remembers the California riots against the Chinese who came to build the railways many years ago, and the deep feeling against the Japanese who followed them, it is possible to point with equal pride to a Japanese-American mayor of San Jose—Norman Y. Mineta.

Rudyard Kipling once described the American as "cosmopolitanly planned." A glimpse at the names in the United States Senate indicates the present truth of that phrase: an Aiken, a Brooke, a Fong, a Hruska, an Inouye, a Javits, a Kennedy, a Magnuson, a Montoya, a Pastore, a Schweiker. The American's ancestors may have come here centuries ago to rule broad acres in Virginia, or till them as slaves; they may have begun, a few generations ago, as pedlars along the frontier, or as contract laborers in the cane fields of Hawaii. But the American way is an open way, and where obstacles are raised, they may be overcome.

For change—two hundred years ago or today—does not frighten the American. It is a part of himself, and of his heritage. Change, to the American, is a chance to improve his lot and that of his neighbor. And change is still possible within every institution that has been created here, from government under the Constitution to the bylaws of the local Parent-Teachers Association.

Americans are deeply concerned with social issues at this point in our history, and this concern bodes well for the future. Zbigniew Brzezinski, director of the Research Institute on Communist Affairs at Columbia University, discussed these current trends in a recent article: ". . . contemporary America is demonstrating today its flexibility and adaptability, not rigidity and stagnation. Change is always too rapid for some and too slow for others. Yet, in such areas as poverty, race relations, education and social mores, the reality of the last decade has been that of positive change, and that change is continuing."

What needs to be done, in other words, the American people can do and will do.

United States Capitol, Washington, D.C.

Developing the land and building the cities

The wild and rugged continent, over the centuries, has been tamed.
Land has been cleared and homes have been built.
Some of our people still live in peaceful little country villages.
Many more have gathered in mighty cities whose shining towers
of steel and glass soar to the skies, challenging the darkness.

Lyndon, Vermont   New York City

The rolling farmland of Wisconsin
supports the nation's largest dairy herds and
produces vast quantities of feed for them—
including hay, alfalfa, and oats. West Virginia
ranks first among the states in coal production,
mining about 25 percent of the U.S. total.
It is also rich in history. Harpers Ferry, the site
of John Brown's daring raid in 1859, is now
a National Historical Monument.

Monroe County in southern Wisconsin

Harpers Ferry, West Virginia

Each of our cities has its own unique identity, shaped by history, by the people who settled there, and by the nature of the surrounding area. New Orleans, founded by the French in 1718, is a great seaport and oil center. It is famous for its Mardi Gras and as the cradle of jazz. Denver, the mile-high city near the foothills of the Rockies, was settled during a gold strike in 1859. The Chicago area was a center for wagon trains in the 1830s, is the nation's second largest city as well as an industrial, agricultural, and transportation center.

French Quarter in New Orleans, Louisiana

Denver, capital of Colorado

Chicago, Illinois, on the shores of Lake Michigan

Boston, capital of Massachusetts

Los Angeles, California, with Hollywood Bowl in right foreground

A golden spike, in 1869, completed the railroad that linked
the West to the thriving cities of the East. Founded by Spaniards in 1781,
Los Angeles is today the third most populous city in the United States,
and a center of the aircraft industry. Boston, founded by Puritans in
1630, was the hub of our Revolution and is now one of our greatest
historical and educational centers.

Gateway Arch
in St. Louis is
630 feet high.

2

A Society of Consumers

In the beginning the great American challenge was open space—the original colonists found a vast expanse of land waiting to be explored, settled, developed. For more than three hundred years, as increasing numbers of immigrants reached the shores of the beautiful land, the frontier moved westward. Thousands upon thousands of pioneers crossed the Mississippi at St. Louis, the "Gateway to the West," but there were never enough people to utilize the resources which the land held in such tantalizing abundance. So, to the challenge of space, America responded with the miracle of technology—a technology that would produce a gross national product of a trillion dollars by 1971.

To most of us such a figure is incomprehensible, but what it means in terms of living standards is something else again. The overall average annual income per person in the U.S. today is almost $4,000 (in India it is $79). The average mean income per American family in 1970 was $11,100. Measured in constant dollars, it rose by about a third between 1960 and 1970. Home ownership, an index of economic stability and a promise of social stability, has also been rising. In 1970, 64 percent of all dwelling units in the United States were occupied by their owners—an increase of almost 50 percent since 1940.

In real terms of buying power, the typical American family is paid more than families in any other major country. The American industrial worker works one hour to buy a specific meal for a family of four; in Denmark—the European nation that comes closest to the American standard—the average worker has to spend nearly an hour and a half to earn the same meal. In West Germany and Britain that meal costs more than two hours of work, and in Italy—almost five hours. In

1970, the typical American family spent 17 percent of its take-home pay for food; in Britain the figure was 30 percent; and in the Soviet Union it was 50 percent. An American worked only 45 minutes to earn a steak that cost a Russian more than three hours of labor; and he could buy a refrigerator to keep it in for less than an average week's pay, as against more than a month's pay for the Russian. As a matter of fact, just about the only ordinary thing the Russian can buy for less time worked is a haircut! In Moscow it takes him only 39 minutes to earn one; for the New Yorker, it takes 46 minutes.

Perhaps the most significant gain of all is the fact that most Americans now belong economically to the middle class. Traditionally, the distribution of wealth has been described as a pyramid—the tiny apex representing the rich and the broad base, the poor. In this country today it should be drawn as a square standing on one of its points. At the top are the 2.3 percent of families with incomes of $25,000 or more, at the bottom are the 20 percent of families with incomes under $4,600. In the great area between these two extremes are the 77.7 percent who are neither rich nor poor—the middle class. Furthermore, an average blue-collar operative or craftsman earned only slightly less at the end of the past decade than an average professional or manager had earned at the beginning. The blue collar man, in short, has joined the middle class.

Many Americans also own stock—they have capital invested in American industry. There were 31 million individual shareholders in 1970, as compared with 20 million in 1965 and 6.5 million in 1952. The number of savings accounts increased by 39 million during the same period. In one way or another, more Americans are sharing in the rewards of the nation's economic affluence than ever before.

Today the land has been transformed. It shelters nearly 210 million people, and has given them an abundance that has dazzled the world. This achievement was due only in part to the richness of the land—rich though it was and is. When we founded this nation, other countries were stronger, more developed, and as richly endowed as America. But we had something they did not have—a concept of freedom which permitted the individual to follow his own dreams, alone or in voluntary association with his fellows. The rigid controls imposed by state, church, and class which hindered the development of so many countries did not exist in the new land. The individual was free to move out to the frontier, to build his home, and to create a new society.

At first, the great empty spaces had to be opened up—roads, canals, railroads, and bridges were needed to span the continent. Later there would be the telegraph, the telephone, radio, television, and the airplane to knit it all together. But even when the stream of immigrants

A sale on bread in Cleveland—buyer plans to put it in his home freezer. Below, green beans are quick-frozen: refrigerator trucks are loaded up for market. At right, combines harvest wheat near Walla Walla, Washington.

swelled to a torrent, the country was plagued with a chronic labor shortage. Americans were a pragmatic people, they were willing to try anything—and to make it work. They found their answers in technology, welcoming and nourishing it here as nowhere else.

It was no accident, therefore, that an American, Robert Fulton, developed a practical steamboat; that the first link of Samuel F. B. Morse's telegraph was between the nation's capital and Baltimore; that Alexander Graham Bell's telephone and Lee de Forest's vacuum tube first carried voices and flashed living pictures through American space; that the Wright brothers made their first flight from an American beach. The railroad was not invented here, but Americans had flung a line across their continent nearly half a century before the Russians pushed the Trans-Siberian across to the Pacific.

Nor is it surprising that Eli Whitney helped clothe a world cheaply with his cotton gin, or that Cyrus McCormick, whose reaper opened the vast prairies for the economical growth of cereal grains, became one of the founders of the age of technological agriculture. Even today, when these innovations are common property around the world, the harvest from one out of four acres of U.S. croplands is exported to some 150 countries, while we eat extremely well from the remainder.

The industrial revolution began in England while the American Revolution was aborning. In fact, England's reluctance to allow industrial development in its colonies was a powerful impetus to America's decision to revolt. But it was Eli Whitney who helped lay the foundation for true mass production by the use of interchangeable parts, and it was Henry Ford, many years later, whose development of the assembly line was the basis for the mass production of highly complex manufactures. The genius of these and other Americans completely revised the profile of American society. Today, with only 4.8 percent of the population on farms, the United States is the world's largest food products exporter. Despite the fact that ours is the first industrialized country in the world to employ more than half its work force in services, rather than in farming and manufactures, we are still the greatest industrial producer the world has ever known.

These changes in patterns of production were reflected in patterns of distribution. Americans were the first to appreciate the fact that only mass consumption can support mass production. Robert Ingersoll preached the concept, and proceeded to prove it by amassing a fortune with a good, cheap watch known as "the watch that made the dollar famous." Cross-grained, hard-headed Henry Ford went a step farther. He not only made the Model-T—the inexpensive transportation that put a nation on wheels—but in early 1914 astonished the world by raising

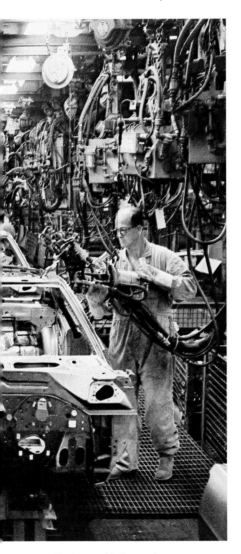

Ford assembly lines today are more sophisticated than those that produced the Model T. A Ford first came off the original line in 1913.

average wages in his plant from about $2.40 for a nine-hour day to a minimum of $5.00 for an eight-hour day. Why he did it, Henry Ford did not say. There was no union at Ford for another quarter of a century, nor any special labor scarcity to pressure the move. The United States, in fact, was enduring a recession at the time. But the end result of the Ford initiative—in production methods, in appraisal of the market, in wages—did very much to establish that peculiarly American economic phenomenon: the consumer society.

This is neither classic nor Marxist; it seeks to secure the widest possible distribution of goods through mass production of items at prices the greatest possible number of consumers can afford. In the consumer society, the economic rules of Adam Smith—that wages will be as low and prices as high as the market will bear—were no longer considered valid. American technology soon began to deliver a flood of mass-produced goods; ships, trains, and trucks carried them out across the land where rising wages turned laborers into customers. This concept of a consumer society has permitted America to share larger amounts of goods among more people than any other nation in human history.

Until very recently, the magnitude of this achievement blinded most of us to its true costs. As early as the turn of the century, there were people who were alarmed by the heedless exploitation of natural resources. Whole forests had been gutted for lumber, for charcoal and fuel, or simply to clear the land for farming. Vast stores of minerals had been pillaged, leaving only mountains of tailings and ruined countrysides. Conservation was in the air during the days of Theodore Roosevelt, but even dedicated conservationists failed then to see the full dimensions of the problem. Their laudable aim was to conserve some of our most beautiful areas, but Americans were not yet ready to think of the complexity of a whole continental ecology. The droughts and dust storms of the 1930s taught us the results of carelessly disturbing the age-old ecology of the prairies, but developers continued to drain marshlands and farms; factories and cities continued to pour wastes into lakes, rivers, and oceans.

The public paid little heed because our resources seemed inexhaustible. As more and more workers grew rich enough to own a car, highways laced the continent ever tighter, carrying more and more traffic which filled the air with polluting exhausts. When chemistry offered quick ways to eliminate insects and plant diseases, its products were as quickly adopted. When plastics and synthetic fabrics were developed, they were hailed as substitutes for woods and metals, and for the vast acreage required for cotton and sheep. When more and more power was needed, dams that drowned whole valleys were built—and when that was not enough, we thought that atomic energy—or some other technological

miracle—would be able to supply all of our power requirements.

In our eagerness to raise the standard of living of the greatest possible number of people in our consumer society, we failed to realize that the bills—for such simple and supposedly inexhaustible things as air and water—were beginning to pile up. We also neglected to include in the selling price the *true* cost of the goods we produce—the costs of not polluting the air and water in the first place, or of cleaning them up afterwards. And until quite recently, we forgot to include the cost of getting rid of the things we produce once their useful life is over. We simply dumped the trash—someplace else.

Smog—at first only a bad joke about Los Angeles—set city dwellers coughing and turned forests brown; fish deserted filthy lakes and streams, and birds' eggs failed to hatch; beaches were posted as unfit for swimming and swordfish caught in the depths of distant oceans were declared unfit for eating.

By the time Rachel Carson's "Silent Spring" was published, more and more Americans had begun to listen. The book hit the best-seller list. But it was not until the astronauts of Apollo 11 first set foot on the moon that millions of us began to see our environment from a different perspective. Until then, our attitudes still reflected the frontier tradition. Horizons were unlimited and space—prairie space—seemed to be infinite. The astronauts saw the world as none of us had ever seen it before. They travelled beyond any horizon we had ever conceived; they saw—and brought us photographs of—this one beautiful *living* speck in the barren and empty vastness of interplanetary space. We began to realize that not only our country, but also our planet, is finite rather than infinite in its dimensions and its resources. We began to understand that the air we breathe and the water we drink are resources that do not exist on the moon—or anywhere between here and the moon. They are resources—like any other—that can be polluted, exhausted, destroyed.

There have been efforts, in recent years, to find a scapegoat—industry, developers, government—who might be blamed for the mess we have made of our environment. "Why wasn't all this anticipated?" was the question asked by many. One businessman, who owns a huge marina on a polluted lake in Michigan, told *Fortune,* "I don't know. What could we have done? Who's used to coping with problems like this?" An automobile executive, who is now working to redesign his products around antipolluting devices, came up with a different answer: "Issues don't get dealt with until they become issues."

There is no doubt that the environment is now an issue, and that it cannot be resolved until everyone—from the federal government to the individual householder—goes to work on it. All of us are to some degree

Similar sign is posted on Michigan side of state line.

View of the earth from Apollo 10

responsible for environmental problems because all of us have accepted the fruits of technology without thinking much about their costs. A major challenge in the 1970s is to use our technology to improve the quality of our environment. We have discovered at last that nothing—no *thing*—disappears. Things change form, can be moved from here to there. But every thing that was ever on this planet is still here. We have begun to think in terms of recycling and resource recovery and, if history is any guide, chances are that America will lead the world in this area as we have led it in so many others.

In 1970, President Nixon outlined the broad problem: "The time has come for a new quest. A quest not for greater quantity of what we have—but for a new quality of life in America." During the same year, he gathered most of the federal government's antipollution activities into two new agencies. The National Oceanic and Atmospheric Administration is taking the lead in research and development; the Environmental Protection Agency is focusing on establishing standards, on monitoring, and on enforcing controls.

The great corporations and industries that make and use packaging of all kinds—metal, paper, glass, plastic—pooled their resources with labor unions in October of 1970 to fund the nonprofit National Center for Resource Recovery. This organization will coordinate the research which is going on in industry and in municipalities, and will make the results available to anyone who can use them. In Maryland, the Bureau of Mines has recently built a pilot plant that recovers saleable materials from incinerator residue—and can do it at a profit. (The project director fondly calls this residue "urban ore.") In Delaware, a recycling plant being built by a private firm will turn 1,000 tons of refuse into 540 tons of usable products in a day. These are only small beginnings for a nation that daily produces almost 10 million tons of solid waste. But they suggest that we may eventually be able to transform our landslide of trash —using it as a self-replenishing source of raw materials for the production of goods which a growing population will need.

The problems of pollution will plague America for some time to come, but they are not insoluble. Because, as a people, we often tend to emphasize our shortcomings and ignore our successes, it would be well to remember that most countries would like nothing better than to be able to *afford* such problems as these. Underdeveloped countries have precious little to throw away and, of necessity, tend to recycle their wastes. Poor folk do not pollute on the scale of the rich. Ironically, America is suffering from its very success—from the abundance that a free and hardworking people have created in this great land.

It is true, of course, that every American is not rich, that our cur-

rent rate of unemployment is about 6 percent, and that there are poor people in this country. But it is not true that the poor are getting poorer. Whereas 28 percent of all families in 1935 had incomes below what was then considered to be the "subsistence level," the figure fell to about 10 percent by 1970. What is more, our concept of how much a family needs for subsistence rose during these years. In 1935, a subsistence budget, measured in 1971 dollars, was considered to be less than $2,300; by 1971, the amount had risen to about $4,150. Millions of Americans have pulled themselves out of poverty and into the middle class, and we are doing more now than ever before to help those left behind to do the same.

It may be taken as an encouraging development that, in our country, the poor have become visible and audible. In other countries—even in some of the more affluent ones—the plight of the poor has been swept under the carpet and very little is being done about it. As pointed out by *The New York Times,* "surprisingly few countries have launched major social programs like those in the United States, or even acknowledged the scope of the problem." In Greece, for instance, the *Times* reported that no aid is provided to families whose per capita income is $13 a month or more. In Rome, where there are only seven trained social workers, registered poor are given $1.30 per month in coupons plus half as much for each child. In Great Britain, one man in six earns a poverty wage of about $36 per week. In West Germany, a woman with two dependent children may receive as much as $110 per month, but there are few social programs for the unskilled, and a great many people still live in bomb shelters, abandoned barracks, and settlement camps. Statistics are hard to come by because officials often deny that poverty exists.

In our country very few problems can be swept under the rug. And this is good. For problems that are hidden away are less likely to be resolved; they tend to fester, to become infectious. Americans expose and examine the inequities that exist in our society. We make it easy for others to criticize us because we so frequently criticize ourselves. But this, in the long run, serves as a spur to improvement and advancement. When we are challenged by a social, economic, industrial or technological problem, it is in our nature to confront it and to do something about it.

The world looks on, usually unaware that the problems we face today will be theirs to face tomorrow. Pollution is an issue in every industrialized country, but most paid very little attention until it was highly publicized in the United States. Racial discrimination was considered to be an American problem that did not exist in Europe—until it cropped up in Great Britain, France, West Germany, and the Soviet Union. Crimes of violence, which were publicized in America long before the days of Chicago's Al Capone, are suddenly hitting the front page of the

Incinerator residue on conveyor at Maryland pilot plant of U.S. Bureau of Mines, and (below) the "urban ore" which is recovered

staid old *Times* in "safe and sane" London. Such crimes had increased by 5 percent between January and August of 1971, and Scotland Yard officials set off a storm which involved Parliament, the government, and a variety of civil liberties groups by urging a crackdown and harsher treatment for violent criminals.

America has no monopoly on the social problems of the world, but we are certainly trying to deal with them in a responsible fashion. For instance, a *Fortune* survey showed that the heads of companies that did a billion dollars or more of business a year believe that their organizations must be socially responsible, even at the expense of immediate profits. The main point to be emphasized here—and it is a characteristic of the consumer society—is that the executives recognize, as one of them said, that "unless you make a contribution to enhance human values, your institution is in danger." Or, as another put it more bluntly: "There is more in social responsibility than economic gain in the short run. Short run is poor. We have to be in it because of the long-range effect on the company's profits."

To meet this concept of social responsibility—"social change, equal rights, equal opportunities, hard-core unemployed, the whole bit," as one businessman phrased it—is not easy. But business is getting ample instruction from a large number of groups—blacks, women, workers, and consumers—that bring pressure on Congressmen, on institutions and individual stockholders, and directly on boards of directors. Whatever their degrees of enthusiasm or exaggeration, whatever mistakes they may make in detail, such groups as follow the lead of men like Ralph Nader or Saul Alinsky prove two points: that even the most massive institutions are sensitive to public pressure, and that the public, far from being a faceless, voiceless mass, can speak in its own particular interest—and be heard.

More, in the American republic those voices are backed by votes, and in the American consumer society they are backed by dollars. The combination is sometimes awkward to bring to bear, but it is eventually effective, and the individual need not relapse into apathy because of the size of the structures which encompass him. Whether through so prestigious an institution as the Sierra Club fighting a dam site, or a random collection of hard-hats and hippies battling an oil slick in San Francisco Bay, there is room for meaningful action by every American.

This room is being extended, even on the assembly line. Many firms, large and small, are becoming aware of discontent at the factory—a discontent that high wages do not quell, and which causes high turnover, absenteeism, and shoddy workmanship. One of the causes of this discontent is the fact that assembly lines were designed for uneducated or undereducated immigrants, yet most factory workers between the ages of

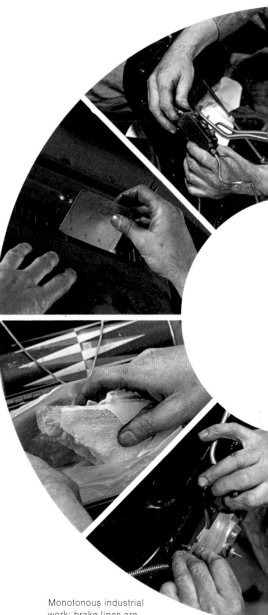

Monotonous industrial work: brake lines are attached to junction blocks 348 times on an 8-hour shift.

25 and 40 today have had twelve years of schooling. Men on the assembly line say they find their work "boring and monotonous," and that they themselves are "just a number" or "just a cog in a machine." Such men are well paid but find that elaboration of corporate structures, the increase in technological innovations, and the accumulation of specialized services tend to take them farther and farther away from the end product. There is no longer very much pride in craftsmanship or in individual creativity and achievement. And white collar workers, increasingly numerous, find themselves to be little better off.

It was during the Revolution that Baron von Steuben, training Washington's ragged army, wrote to a friend in Europe: "You say to your soldier 'Do this' and he doeth it; but I am obliged to say 'This is the reason why you ought to do that' and then he does it!" The American mistrust of authority has always been great; it is not surprising that this mistrust manifests itself in factories today.

Not that the American worker necessarily has to have an order explained to him; it is quite possible that he knows more about the job than the foreman who gives the order. But resentment of authority is rampant, and many employers—an increasing number—recognize the fact. There is a new word abroad in American business today; "job enrichment," meaning greater consultation with individual employees about their jobs, more responsiveness to technical suggestions from them, and in general, an effort to give employees a greater chance to participate in a way that will be more meaningful to them.

Serious efforts along this line still tend to be confined to smaller plants and to the nonunionized. One reason for this latter phenomenon is probably the constant struggle in unionized industries to keep the line between managerial and union prerogatives intact. But those plants that have introduced "job enrichment" (usually although not always under the direction of qualified psychologists) are pleased with the results, both in employee morale and in profits. It is a trend that is virtually sure to be extended and broadened, given the sensitivity of business to the new demand for social responsibility and its growing awareness that the worker is not a number in the accounting department's ledger, any more than the consumer is one in the sales department's computer.

The foregoing indicates that individual aspiration can find outlets among the mass of consumers and the mass of workers, and that the whole concept of "mass" is beginning to break down. The traditional American individualism is today reacting to the spread of huge corporate entities over so much of American industry and merchandising. Such developments and pressures probably hold out the greatest hope for the largest number of Americans within the so-called corporate state.

But there are others. Behind the push button and the punch card lies an intricate and challenging body of knowledge which has by no means reached its limits. Imagination and experimentation—"R & D" (research and development)—is the very heart of American technology, and it is a field in which work is rewarding and stimulating.

Moreover, even in positions which do not, in themselves, provide imaginative stimulus nor the satisfactions of craftsmanship, the greater leisure offered by limited work weeks and earlier retirement affords opportunities for self-realization outside the job that earlier generations did not know. There was not much "job enrichment" possible feeding an open hearth furnace through a twelve-hour day, or sewing fine seams in a sweatshop for the same time span—nor was there much left of the week, or of human energy, when the toil was broken for minimal rest and recuperation. When personal savings, and those of hard-pressed sons and daughters, were the only recourse at retirement, life held all too little promise for the future.

It has recently been calculated that, during the past century, the U.S. worker has gained about 50,000 additional work-free hours over his lifetime. This is the result of reduction of the work week, more holidays and longer vacations, later starts in youth and earlier retirement in age. The figures are complicated by awareness that in 1970, more than 4 million workers, or 5.1 percent of the labor force, held two or more jobs. Overtime, too, is common. Moreover, the very fact of extensive home ownership, plus the vehicles and appliances of affluence and the mobility of the worker, means time spent on maintenance and in commuting.

Nevertheless, leisure has grown, and is taking new forms. The steel industry, for example, in 1963 began giving a "sabbatical" of three months' extra paid vacation every five years to workers in the top half of the seniority roster, and then, in 1968, added three extra weeks' vacation every five years for those with somewhat less seniority. And the practice of working longer hours and fewer days is spreading in some occupations, leaving leisure—and work—concentrated. Early retirement and increased vacation time are bulking larger in union contract demands; vacation time has grown by 50 percent in the decade of the 1960s. But the trend toward a shorter work week—of four or even three days—may not persist. Some experts believe that the ever-increasing demand for services will use up time saved through increased productivity, as well as the production of normal additions to the work force.

It is worth bearing in mind that the "corporate state" does not engage the working days of even a majority of those who work. Economist Victor Fuchs, discussing the "service economy," points out: "Most people do not work and never have worked for a large corporation; most produc-

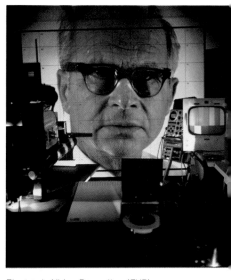

Electronic Video Recording (EVR) was invented by Peter Carl Goldmark at CBS.

Krypton laser at Xerox laboratory (above), and Kodak's tunable continuous-output liquid dye laser (at right)

Data acquisition and display facilities
of ITT at space and missile test center

tion does not take place and never has taken place in large corporations. In the future, the large corporation is likely to be overshadowed by the hospitals, universities, research institutes, government agencies, and professional organizations that are the hallmark of a service economy."

This, it should be pointed out, is a natural characteristic of the consumer society and not the result of any arbitrary selection of such types of work by young people—or their elders—opting for some "Consciousness III" in revolt against the system. But it also implies that newcomers in the labor force will have a wider variety of choices as the service industries grow to embrace the two-thirds of the work force anticipated by 1980, and greater chances of self-development by work than previous generations could ever have known.

And among those choices are the old ones, the adventurous ones that challenged Americans when the land was first being opened to the industrious, the thrifty, and the venturesome. Even corporate giants can be met on their own terms in a world of evolving technology and changing markets and mores. George Eastman, before the turn of the century, had made Kodak a household word (one of the best known trade names anywhere in the world) and the production of cameras and films a great enterprise. But in the 1930s, a student began studying the polarization of light as an applied science. At twenty-eight a Harvard drop-out, he founded the Polaroid Corporation, and before he was forty Edwin Herbert Land had invented a camera which delivered finished photographs seconds after exposure. This, as well as many other commercial applications of the principles of polarized light, built the organization up to present annual sales of more than $425 million.

Individual enterprises on such a scale, of course, are rare—although spin-offs from, say, computer production by major firms have been extensive and profitable. But for those who wish to launch into their own businesses along more modest lines, the opportunities are still great, and the rewards often astonishing to those who believe that big business and high taxes have ended the Horatio Alger epic.

Indeed, new incentives and new methods have developed in our massive economy to encourage the small businessman. Chambers of Commerce have stimulated high school and college students to engage in business ventures—a kind of 4-H Club plan, directed toward commerce and industry rather than the fattening of hogs and the growing of tall corn. The federal government and many state and local governments are ready with advice, instruction, and loans for adults. The service economy itself offers many places in which small enterprises can gain a footing. And several developments within that economy provide men and women, who have plenty of initiative and energy but have failed

65

to accumulate much capital, with the means of starting out on their own.

Prominent among these is the franchise system—old in the world's economy but one that has taken on new life since 1954. Ninety percent of present franchising companies have been founded since 1954, and their number has tripled in the past five years. From the standpoint of the primary producer, franchising is a method of farming out distribution to a large number of outlets. From that of the franchisee, it is a way of getting management and technical advice for his individual enterprise, as well as the advantage of selling a well known and well advertised product within limited territories.

There are about 1,000 franchising companies in the United States today, and about 600,000 franchisees. Forty thousand more of the latter are being added every year. The biggest volume of sales is in automobiles (which were also the first in the franchise field, going back to 1898), with gas stations and tires, and auto parts following in that order. Grocery stores and drive-in food shops are next, followed by soft drinks, hotel-motels, moving companies, coin-operated laundries and dry cleaning establishments, water conditioning services, variety and drug stores —and so on through a wide variety of goods and services. Costs of franchises may be as low as $3,000 or as high as $7,600,000, but most of them are in the intermediate range between $17,000 and $31,000.

This method of starting an individual business is paralleled by another: the leasing of capital goods. This system, in which rentals for the machine hopefully pay for the investment while it does the work, is most conspicuous in the field of automobile and truck rentals, and is widely used for distributing computers, copying machines, and other intricate pieces of business and industrial equipment. Almost everything required for production or transportation can be leased on an annual rental, including, of course, the plant itself and the ground on which it stands. Even social events at home can be supplied with rented dishes and furniture.

Franchise outlet sales account for roughly 10 percent of the gross national product and about a quarter of all retail sales.

So doors are still open in production and merchandizing, no matter how many may seem to have been closed by the growth of mammoth corporations. If the mom-and-pop candy store is vanishing, the mom-and-pop automatic laundry is flourishing in nearly every neighborhood. And if the boy who learns retailing in a local store and goes on to be a great merchant has become one of a vanishing species, there are still ways in which his talents and drive can be put to profitable use.

In spite of the fact that income and estate taxes are high in the United States, the number of millionaires has grown from 27,000 in 1953 to more than 100,000 in 1970. Nobody *likes* to pay taxes, but in this country people believe that it is in everyone's interest to pay his dues to society. Taxes are not, despite occasional conspicuous cases of fraud and evasion, the kind of grim national joke they have become in many countries. A European today might echo the percipient Frenchman, de Tocqueville, in appraising the American's cooperation with the taxing authorities: "Every American has the sense to sacrifice some of his private interests to save the lot. We want to keep, and often lose, the lot."

An example of America's willingness to subordinate private interest to the public good was the support given to the government's efforts to control wages and prices as part of the campaign to combat inflation in 1971-72. No armies of investigators were deployed to enforce compliance—because they were not needed. There were very few cheaters because the population as a whole understood the need to face up to inflation and an unfavorable balance of trade. Most Americans know they have a stake in the general economic health of this country; there are very few here who think of themselves as the downtrodden proletariat so vividly described by Karl Marx. By bringing blue-collar workers into the middle class through the normal processes of the American system, the United States has accomplished the equivalent of what France did when it turned feudal farm laborers into peasant proprietors. But, in France, the change involved a bloody revolution.

There are few "middle Americans" who cannot own their own homes (assisted by mortgage guaranties from the federal government which, incidentally, has insured more than 10 million homes for a total of more than $100 billion since 1934 without costing the taxpayer a penny). These homes, too, are well furnished and equipped with labor-saving devices that make for better eating and better living than was possible when the broom and the ice box were the only household tools for cleaning rooms and preserving perishable foods.

The American middle class has leisure, too, and many means of enjoying it, or profiting by it for self-development in any number of ways, from touring to the local drama club, from golf to a summer session at a nearby college. And leisure can be used for more concrete goals: for organizing political power to seek governmental goals, for organizing the power of consumers to influence corporations. The system is flexible; it provides the opportunity for expressing desires and seeing them met, the ability to effect change or constructively to meet whatever change may be externally imposed.

People often ask why, if Americans can land on the moon, they cannot purge Lake Erie of its pollution, or New York City of its ghettos. The answer is simple enough: the factors involved in traveling through space are almost wholly material; stresses and thrusts can be calculated in advance and the effects of gravity, or lack of gravity, foreseen and guarded against. The human elements are relatively few, highly trained and disciplined for specific tasks, and for the eventualities of equipment failures. This does not detract from the skill and courage of the men involved, nor has it prevented accidents that are costly in lives and treasure. But it is, in effect, a laboratory situation that can be reduced to computerized data and very precisely controlled.

For Lake Erie or the ghetto, the data are fluctuating and uncertain because of the human factors involved in each. The depths of human greed and the heights of human devotion have never been capsulized into a formula, and the precise balance of conflicting human needs is not susceptible to analysis by test tube or computer. What America does possess is tremendous vitality, technical equipment, and scientific knowledge; an excess of time, energy, and goods beyond mere subsistence; the capability to mobilize the public will; and adaptable institutions. These and many other factors will enable us to resolve such problems as pollution, crime, poverty. We can do so, too, in an atmosphere of individual initiative and group cooperation that will enhance personal, ethnic, and class self-esteem, rather than diminish them all to some collection of numerals on a punch card.

And we *are* facing and resolving the problems which confront us—

The good life for "middle Americans" includes a chance to own their own homes (Daly City, Cal.), plenty of home-cooked food (Gloucester, Mass.) and time to read uncensored newspapers (Atlanta, Ga.).

however clumsy and slow the process may seem to those impatiently aware of current shortcomings, however illogical to those who have some patent theory of instant reconstruction of the human condition. Dr. George Hay Brown, Director of the Census, describes the emerging typical American in these words: "More prosperous; better educated; a resident of the suburbs; for many, agricultural days behind them. They will live in better housing, have more discretionary purchasing power and be more discriminating in what they buy."

Somewhat wryly, Dr. Brown added: "We have survived many threats to our national well-being and I see no reason to believe that we cannot survive prosperity—particularly since it brings with it the means to achieve our ends."

69

The abundance produced by a hardworking people

Total output of goods and services in the U.S. today
has passed the trillion dollar mark, exceeding the combined output
of Western Europe and Japan. Our steel industry, a basic component
of the economy, produces about a fifth of the world's steel—more
than any other country. In 1969, the nation's 857,000 iron and steel
workers earned wages totalling $7.7 billion.

Blast furnace in
Ashland, Kentucky

Rolls of sheet steel ready for shipment to Detroit, Michigan

Steel bar, heated to 2,200°F, is shaped by "big-hammer man."

71

About 109 million cars, trucks and buses are registered in the U.S. In 1970, 82 percent of all families owned cars (including the 29 percent who owned two or more); 8.3 million new cars and 11.5 million used cars were purchased; retail sales for vehicles, tires, batteries, accessories and gas stations totalled $90 billion. In 1967, the last year for which figures are available, more than 2 million people were employed in wholesale and retail sales of motor vehicles, gasoline, accessories, and equipment, and in services such as repairs, parking and rentals—in addition to the 739,000 then employed in manufacturing vehicles and equipment.

New autos are driven onto ramplike panels of new railcars, specially designed by General Motors and the Southern Pacific. Panels are then raised, and 30 Vegas fit snugly and safely inside—nose down.

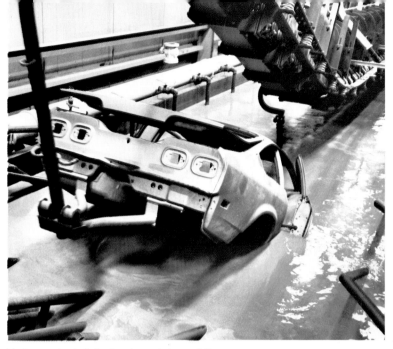

Anti-corrosion bath is given to car before painting. Carpets and seats are installed.

Car is tested on road simulator (below) under huge vents that remove exhausts.

Skilled hands and years of experience are still needed, but much of the work once done by craftsmen is now completely mechanized. New skills are required to operate and maintain complex new equipment, but the engraver's craft is one that never goes out of style. The picture engraver working on a postage stamp (bottom right) is one of only twelve who make all the engravings for U.S. stamps, currency, and bonds.

"First hand" on papermaking machine adjusts flow of pulp and water.

Man working at printing press is skilled and well paid.

Digital electrometer is assembled at Corning Glass. To improve employee morale, assembly-line techniques have been abandoned. This worker does the whole job; profits are up, rejects are down.

Skilled glass blower makes special components for TV camera tubes at RCA.

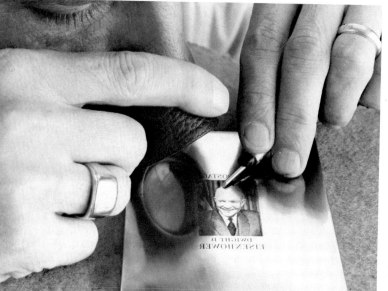

The abundance of food produced on our farms is the result of efficient use of advanced agricultural techniques. In 1920, 30 percent of our people had to farm 956 million acres to feed a population of only 106 million. In 1970, with only 4.8 percent of our people on farms, we produced more than enough to feed double the population, using only 165 million more acres than fifty years before. We are one of the world's biggest exporters of food, with a 28.5 percent share of wheat exports, 56.3 percent of corn exports, and 94.4 percent of soybean exports.

Tasseling corn on a farm in Lancaster County, Pa. is part of a bumper crop. U.S. produces 43 percent of the world's corn.

Purple grapes are harvested in California. Farm marketing of fruits, vegetables, and nuts in 1970 brought farmers nearly $4.9 billion—10 percent of cash receipts for all farm products.

Irrigation is one of the reasons for high yields per acre.

Rounding up strays on a ranch in Oklahoma: there are 115 million head of cattle in the U.S. valued at more than $21 billion.

Half the horses bred today are used for riding and racing. The rich pastures shown below are part of Calumet Farm, Lexington, Ky. where many Derby winners have been raised.

About 214 million cattle, sheep, lambs,
hogs, pigs, and milk cows are currently
being raised on American farms, for a civilian
population whose per capita annual consumption
of meat is about 185 lbs. Per capita
consumption of fluid milk and cream is about
260 lbs. There are only about 8.3 million horses
in the U.S. today, compared with more than
21 million in 1915, and less than half of
them are used for farm work.

Ewes grazing in Colorado

Fresh produce is hauled to roadside store.

Tuttle store is managed by Hugh's wife, Joan,
who oversees sales crew posed behind the owners.

Nation's oldest family farm is irrigated
with water from pond dug twenty years ago.
Most other farmers in the area have
sold their land as real estate.

Ten generations have farmed this land in Dover, New Hampshire, since the 1630s. When supermarkets began killing off the small stores that bought Hugh Tuttle's fruits and vegetables, he hired a marketing expert and opened his own store. His spread covers 245 acres, 50 of them cultivated, and his store handles up to 1,000 customers a day. They are willing to pay somewhat more for the quality and variety which are Tuttle specialties.

Agribusiness today is big business and the efficiency of
U.S. farm operations and marketing is unmatched in the world.
In the quarter century since the end of World War II, the farm population
decreased by 60 percent—from 24.4 million in 1945 to only 9.7 million
in 1970—and there are only half as many farms today as there were in 1945.
The total number of acres of land in farms (1.1 billion) is about the
same as in 1945, but the average number of acres per farm has
doubled—from 191 acres in 1945 to 383 acres in 1970.

Lettuce-packing apparatus at Salinas, Cal. enables 26 workers to do the work of 45. Each head is wrapped in polystyrene film, conveyed through heat tunnel that shrinks film and keeps lettuce fresh for 16 to 20 days.

Tomatoes (above) are sorted and crated by gloved workers. Mobile carrot-packing plant at Salinas (left) needs 70 workers, can harvest, wash, wrap and pack three railroad carloads of carrots a day.

Demand for electric power is expected to double
in the next decade, and may well outrun production capacity.
We already produce and consume about a third of the world's
electric energy, but there is growing sensitivity to the
pollution and environmental damage power production can cause.
New plant construction has often been stopped or delayed by the
protests of citizen groups, and technology has not yet found
a way to produce ample power without damaging the environment.
Because demand is soaring and time is running out, we may
have to limit consumption, or decide what matters to us
most—unlimited power or a cleaner environment.

Nuclear power plants still produce only
2 percent of U.S. power.

Pump-storage system under construction in
Massachusetts. Water pumped to reservoir in period of
low demand runs back down to produce peak-period power.

New York Power Pool control room dispatchers monitor
power distribution among pool's 8 systems, arrange
peak-period sales of power for members and neighboring pools.

Grand Coulee Dam
in Washington is one
of world's largest
hydroelectric plants.

A quarter of the world's coal is mined in the U.S. and reserves are ample. But not enough new mines have been opened because utilities were eager to invest in nuclear power and refused to sign long-term coal contracts, and because of growing demand for energy sources that are less polluting. Coal, which fuels 46.4 percent of our generation of electric energy, is now in short supply, while 10 percent of production is exported under long-term contracts. Thousands of badly-needed hopper cars (left) sometimes back up at Hampton Roads, Va., waiting to be loaded for shipment abroad.

To carry our electric power, 220,000 miles of high-tension lines have been built. Thousands of square miles of additional land will be needed if power requirements quadruple as expected by the turn of the century.

In "The Geysers" field near San Francisco, wells were vented to test underground steam. They are now capped and the natural steam is piped to turbines that power nation's only operating geothermal installation.

Planes loading at San Francisco International Airport

Freighter escorted by tugs in Baltimore Harbor

Transportation of freight within the United States
is handled 41 percent by rail, 22 percent by oil pipelines,
21 percent by motor vehicles, and 16 percent on inland
waterways including the Great Lakes. The volume of intercity
passenger traffic is carried 87 percent by private cars,
10 percent by airlines, 2 percent by bus, and 1 percent by rail.

Barges on the St. Lawrence Seaway

Freight train crosses Montana.

The communications network that links
the nation includes more than 3.7 million
miles of rural and urban roads and streets.
Almost all households have radios, 95 percent
have TV sets, and 92 percent have telephones.
The net paid circulation of daily newspapers
exceeds 62 million, and the circulation
of business, general and farm periodicals
is about 385 million.

Testing telephone cables in Baltimore, Md.

TV cameraman uses portable,
battery-operated equipment

Highway bridge over the Chesapeake Bay

Freeway interchange in Los Angeles

About 80 million civilians were employed toward the end of 1971—approximately 50 million men and 30 million women. The per capita gross national product in the U.S. is by far the highest in the world—$4,664. Sweden, with $3,315, is the only other country that exceeds $3,000. The average weekly wage of a production worker in manufacturing is $140, and annual per capita income in the U.S. is now about $4,000.

Working in the oil fields

No sale at the lunch counter

Lining up the job with a surveyor's level

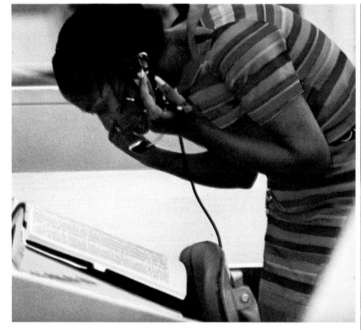

Directory assistance operator,
Baltimore, Md.

Overseas telephone operator, Pittsburgh, Pa.

The harried housewife at right, according to government statisticians, is not considered to be in the country's labor force. This, however, does not mean she works less hard than the man who chops down a tree with an axe, or those who manage the nation's business with their brains. There are nearly 35 million housewives like this young woman, and their occupation is probably more time-consuming, and at least as nerve-racking, as any job done by people who are considered to be *in* the labor force.

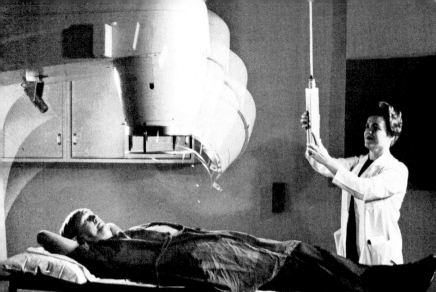

Multiple exposure shows 6-million-volt linear electron accelerator being positioned to bombard internal cancers with high energy x-rays.

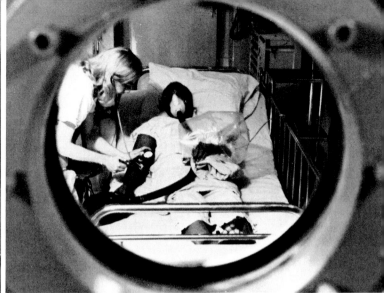

Hyperbaric chamber can quadruple atmospheric pressure forcing oxygen into blood and tissues to kill gangrene bacilli and other infections, and for certain cardiovascular operations.

Advanced medical technology involves
the use of expensive equipment, which partially
explains the soaring cost of hospital care.
The hyperbaric pressure chamber at left, for
instance, cost $800,000 six years ago, and to
maintain and operate it costs $550,000 a year.

Colorimeter measures blood content of 12 substances. It can test
720 samples an hour, printing out biochemical profiles of each.

Neurosurgeon in operating room implants electrode in brain of patient.
Biophysicist at left panel controls radio waves that flash through electrode,
burning out brain cells to cure tremors of Parkinson's disease. Biophysicist
at right panel monitors patient's condition on electroencephalograph.

Console outside hyperbaric chamber monitors patient's vital functions.

The space program which put the first man on the surface of the moon was a miracle of technology that demonstrates what a free society can do when faced with an almost impossible challenge. Private industry, the government and the military, ordinary citizens who willingly paid the bills—all *in combination* succeeded in putting courageous astronauts on the moon and, with the help of the technicians at NASA, in bringing them safely home again.

Man first steps onto surface of the moon on July 20, 1969.

Almost everyone watches moon voyages on their own TV screens at home.

Moon buggy (Lunar Roving Vehicle) was first used by crew of Apollo 15 on July 31, 1971.

Apollo 11 blasts off Cape Kennedy pad on way to the moon.

Town houses in
Town Park Village,
Miami, Florida

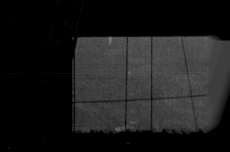

More than $91 billion in new construction was put in place in 1970. There were almost 1.5 million new housing starts; most of them are privately owned, and 815,000 are single-unit structures that cost an average of $18,325 each. Mortgages were taken out on 84 percent of new privately-owned, one-family houses, 16 percent were paid for outright.

In 1830, what was to be Chicago had 20 log cabins. Today, buildings like this one are going up all over town.

About 415,000 mobile homes were built in 1970, compared with only about 63,000 in 1950. The total of these homes in 1970 was more than 1.8 million. A 1969 survey showed that 48 percent of all new homes were mobile homes; that they accounted for 94 percent of new homes under $15,000, 79 percent of those under $20,000, and 67 percent of those under $25,000.

Mobile homes along the Pacific near Santa Monica, California

Two 12-foot sections are bolted together at Lake Park, some are as long as 70 feet, have air conditioners and dishwashers.

Lake Park is a mobile home community in Yorba Linda, California with a lake (right), a clubhouse, and a swimming pool.

103

Nearly 40 million Americans own their own homes,
an increase of 100 percent in the last quarter century. Their
houses may be situated among the trees in suburban Columbia, Maryland,
(below), or close-packed like those in Detroit (bottom right).
Or they may be somewhere in rural America, where the daily trip to
cross-roads mailboxes is still something to look forward to.

Open space, where children
may play without worrying about
speeding cars, is at a premium in
run-down sections of the inner cities.
But new housing developments, for
people in every income bracket,
provide light and air and room
for the youngsters.

Middle-income apartments have playgrounds—and things to climb on.

Low-cost housing development in Washington, D.C.

Housing tract on the peninsula below San Francisco

New towns like Reston, Virginia, provide a mix of apartments and single-family houses for people whose incomes are limited, as well as for those who are more affluent.

3

Americans at Play

mericans have always been a sociable people. We laugh easily; we get all worked up when the home team scores a touchdown or hits a home run; we are quick to call each other by our first names.

We have worked hard to build this nation, but—somehow—we always manage to mix work with play. In the early days, a dawn-to-dusk barn-raising would be followed by a barbecue and a hoe-down. Because the land was spacious and the people were few—and because distances were measured in terms of how far a horse could travel in a day—any excuse to get together was a good excuse for a celebration. Hospitality, on the frontier, was taken for granted. There were no strangers in this land. When someone rode through in an era that did not yet know radio or television—and when newspapers were available only in major cities— he brought news of family and friends from across the mountain, and of the outside world as well. He was welcomed and looked after until the time came for him to ride on again.

Even today, when so much has changed, Americans tend to be easy and cordial when they meet someone they do not know. Visitors from abroad almost invariably use the word "friendly" to describe encounters with ordinary people on their travels through the United States.

They may be somewhat mystified, of course, if they happen to be here when the World Series is underway because everyone speaks strangely of pirates and orioles, and seems either to be glued to a television set or out at the ball park. About 30 million people attend major league baseball games each year, and some 40 million turn out for football—30 million of them at the nation's colleges and universities. Profes-

sional basketball draws about 5 million, high school and college games attract millions more. Horseracing leads every other sport, with attendance estimated at about 70 million, and greyhound racing brings out almost 13 million. But in spite of the fact that these two sports boast of higher attendance figures, ball games are still by far the most popular. No one has been able successfully to estimate how many millions of people spend how many billion hours each year watching such games on TV, but a record-breaking 90 million viewed the World Series in 1971, and there is no doubt at all that this is America's favorite pastime.

This does not mean, however, that Americans take all their sports sitting down. If television were excluded, the doers would probably outnumber the watchers. People who spend weekdays in office or factories show a restless yearning to do something out-of-doors. In ever-increasing numbers, they head for golf courses, tennis courts, beaches, mountains, rivers, lakes, campsites, and national parks. On ordinary weekends, when there is not enough time to travel very far, Americans are usually to be found in their own back yards. We spend nearly $1.5 billion on flowers, seeds, and potted plants each year, and the National Council of State Garden Clubs—the largest association of its kind in the nation—has 14,500 clubs and more than 373,000 members. We also have more than 1 million swimming pools in the United States—many are privately owned and can be reached by simply stepping out the back door. In 1970, we spent more than $35 billion on recreation, excluding the additional billions paid out for such things as travel, food, and lodging.

Americans have not only more money to spend but also more time for leisure than ever before. People retire earlier and live longer, and there are more three-day weekends as a result of congressional action changing several holidays so that they fall on Mondays. The number of vacation weeks enjoyed by workers has also increased—by 50 percent over the past decade, and by 176 percent in the last quarter century.

Golf and tennis are increasingly popular, though for a great many years both sports were the province of the rich. There are about 11 million tennis players using some 100,000 outdoor courts—in 1971, nearly 2 million adults bought tennis rackets, and more than 3 million bought tennis balls. More than 12 million played golf in 1971, as against only 3.2 million in 1950. Only 15 percent now play on private courses; the rest pay a nominal fee on courses that are open to the public.

Years ago, when pioneers began the trek westward, hunting and fishing were prime sources of food for the table. Today, since we raise our meat and buy our fish—sometimes fresh, usually frozen or canned—hunting and fishing are considered as sports. Millions take time off from work to be there when the "season" opens on whatever fish or game may be available nearby. Nearly 52 million licenses—30 million for fishing and 22 million for hunting—are taken out each year. Among the 18 million visitors to national wildlife refuges, however, birdwatching, photography, and auto touring are more popular than hunting or fishing.

Bicycling, like hunting and fishing, did not begin as a sport. Fathers went to work and mothers went shopping—on pedal-powered wheels. Children who now ride buses went to school in the same way. Then, with the advent of mass transportation and Henry Ford's Model T, bicycles became toys for the youngsters. But, unlike hunting and fishing, bicycling may again turn into a practical means of transportation. Some 80 million people ride bicycles today, twice as many as ten years ago. Most of them still ride for pleasure and exercise, but an increasing number do so for other reasons. "I got sick and tired of sitting in endless, noxious traffic jams," one biker explained to *U.S. News & World Report,* "I found that I could actually get to work in less time by cycling than by driving. Besides that, I am getting tremendous exercise and feel better for it."

This irritation with clogged highways, combined with the fact that more and more Americans feel the need for exercise, is confirmed by government statisticians. In 1960, pleasure driving was our favorite outdoor recreational activity. By 1965, however, the Bureau of Outdoor Recreation estimated that our 940 million pleasure drives were lagging behind our 970 million pleasure swims, and pleasure walks for thirty minutes or more had assumed a commanding lead—there were 1 billion of them. This makes one stop and think—not about the obvious pleasures of hiking, but about the problems of conducting a survey that will provide such statistics as these.

An easier figure to verify, perhaps, is the fact that, in 1970, some 200,000 people hiked along parts of the Appalachian Trail—extending 2,000 miles from Maine to Georgia. Equally popular is the Pacific Crest Trail, which runs along mountain ranges from Mexico to Canada.

Although most of us take vacations in the summer, more and more people are heading for the mountains in winter. There are about 6 million skiers in the United States who spend more than $1 billion on travel, accommodations, tow charges, and equipment. Ice skating and coasting cost almost nothing at all. Youngsters and grownups will be found by the million, wherever the weather is right and there are farm ponds and hillsides, canals and lakes, steeply sloping village roads, and open areas in the parks of our cities.

It is in summer, however, that the migration of vacationers becomes something of a stampede. They go to the mountains, to the seashore, and to national and state parks and recreation areas. Some 45

Millions of vacationing Americans take camping trips every summer, and on weekends bicycling provides recreation for the whole family.

skiers on chairlift at Whitefish, Montana

million enjoy yearly camping expeditions, and 44 million took more than one recreational boating trip during 1970. Millions of ordinary Americans now travel abroad—something only the rich could afford in earlier generations. More than 5 million spent time in foreign countries in 1970, as against only 676,000 just two decades ago.

But most of us do our touring at home. In a year, Americans take 160 million pleasure trips that cover at least 100 miles, or involve at least one night away from home. A typical vacationing family is gone for about two weeks and travels less than 200 miles, although many drive 2,000 or more. Ninety percent of families on holiday use a car, creating traffic jams of monumental proportions. One summer traveller from the East was astounded, in 1971, to find himself caught in bumper-to-bumper traffic while crossing Loveland Pass—one of the most breathtaking roads in the Rockies. "It was," he commented, "just like the trip home from the beaches of Delaware or Maryland on a Sunday night in August."

It is not often that bad, however, because even today a third of the nation's land area is still publicly owned. State parks cover more than 8.5 million acres in 3,337 areas, and total reported visits increased from 259 million in 1960 to 415 million a decade later. The national park system includes nearly 30 million acres in 281 areas. The most famous of these are the thirty-five national parks, which were visited by 182 million people in 1971. Although facilities were badly strained by the ever-increasing demand, the parks managed to accommodate 16 million overnight stays, 9 million of them by campers.

The parklands of America reflect the extraordinary beauty and diversity of our country. Visitors may range through deep forests of spruce and pine in Maine or the mighty sequoise of California; they may watch the acquatic wildlife in the Everglades of Florida or drive among stark, red rock castles in the Canyonlands of Utah; they may ponder the beauty of snowcapped Tetons in Wyoming, or marvel at molten lava flowing from a volcano in Hawaii.

Yellowstone, covering 3,472 square miles, is the oldest of our national parks—celebrating its centennial in 1972. It offers facilities for camping, hiking, horseback riding, scenic drives, fishing, and evening programs around outdoor campfires. There are waterfalls, geysers, and canyons, and an abundance of wildlife—including one of the "endangered species," the grizzly bear. Another extraordinarily scenic region is the Rocky Mountain National Park in Colorado, with 107 named peaks soaring higher than 10,000 feet, and bighorn sheep which share the protected area with hundreds of other species of wildlife. There are thousands of islands, too, from the Aleutians of Alaska to Chincoteague off the coast of Virginia. For the naturalist, there is the winter sanctuary for

113

Birdwatcher in Illinois finds five
infant field sparrows in a grass nest.

our endangered whooping cranes—the Aransas National Wildlife Refuge—a 54,000-acre reserve that also provides peace for more than 300
other types of birds. And there the mile-deep Grand Canyon, in Arizona,
a mecca for tourists from at home and abroad.

In addition to the stunning natural beauty of our parklands,
there is a broad range of tourist attractions to enthrall the wandering
American. He can live in the horse-and-buggy world of Mackinac Island
in Michigan; watch cowboys round up cattle bound for the world's largest livestock market in Omaha, Nebraska; enjoy the sight of herds of buf-

falo, deer, and elk running free in the Badlands National Monument of South Dakota; thrill to the excitement of the country's largest rodeo at Cheyenne, Wyoming; walk the streets of Virginia City in Nevada, the restored ghost town that flourished in the gold rush of the 1860s; spend the night in Colonial Williamsburg, where the buildings and way of life of the eighteenth century has been recreated down to the smallest detail. He can pan for gold high in the Rockies, join an archeological dig in the ruins of an ancient Indian village in the Southwest, or ride a cowpony on a dude-ranch in Wyoming.

For the adventurous, there is surfing, skydiving, drag racing, and mountain climbing. For the exceptional athlete, there may be a chance to make an Olympic team—the United States has been the unofficial winner in fourteen of the seventeen Olympic games held since 1896. For those who need to lose a little weight, there's jogging and bowling, or a workout at the local gym. Some people play bridge, gin rummy or chess; others find pleasure in a book, at the theater or in a concert hall.

And for the American who is looking for something new in entertainment, there is Walt Disney World in Florida, on a 28,000-acre site that attracted thousands of visitors each day during its three-day opening in 1971. There are hundreds of thousands of playgrounds, large and small, but this one—which expects 10 million visitors a year—is bound to be the biggest of them all. But Americans do not have to travel to Florida—or to any other special place—to make the most of their leisure time. More people go to the local zoo, for instance, than attend all the stadiums that feature our most popular spectator sports, and there is no way to count the number of picnic baskets packed and transported to local parks.

There are also chores to be done in our leisure time—particularly for the 40 million American families who own their own homes. There are lawns to be seeded, weeded, and mowed; there are bushes to be planted and hedges to be trimmed; and there are millions of cars to be washed on city streets or in the driveways of suburbia.

Walt Disney World in Florida

There are simple pleasures, too, that every family can enjoy on summer weekends—or at twilight after work. In the towns and cities, people sit out on front porches or stoops to chat awhile with neighbors, while the children jump rope, play hopscotch or stickball. In suburbia, families tend to eat outdoors when summer evenings are long, and fathers get out with youngsters after lighting the charcoal in back yard barbecues. They throw baseballs and footballs—or just enjoy the fun of romping around together on the grass. On farms in rural areas, mothers get things ready for early-morning starts, and fathers may work again until dark. But the heat of day is over and the evening star is bright— and the sounds of playing children carry out across the fields.

Time to spare for simple pleasures

Recreation is a family affair for most Americans.
Vacation time has increased 176 percent since 1946 and three-day
weekends are the rule for most holidays. When the snow flies up north
everyone has to bundle up, but there are always snowmen to build,
there are skating and skiing, and sleds to ride. In places like Florida,
it's one long summer vacation for the youngsters, and even their
parents spend most of their spare time outdoors.

The Ellis family lives in Tampa and frequently goes
camping on weekends in a nearby county park that offers
fishing, boating and miles of open beaches.

Just being together is something special when father gets home from work—and the little girl in Georgia just can't wait to try on that hard hat of his. There's companionship on mountain trails, and fun on sandy beaches. But to the city-bound pair on New York's lower east side, it's quite enough to share the end of an Italian street festival. Out in Colorado, it's hard to tell who's proudest of whom, but the football player and his master-machinist dad are obviously having a very good day.

119

Life begins for a young family in Maine, where a young mother spends a quiet moment with her sturdy young son. It draws to a close for the old gentleman below, whose children and grandchildren get together to celebrate his ninety-third birthday—with a banquet and a homemade cake.

The covered wagons of today no longer form a circle for defense against the Indians, but the trailer caravan (below) settles in for the night in very much the same way. They have assembled in Great Falls, Montana, before heading into Canada for a 61-day, 5,100-mile trip to British Columbia and Alaska. In Albuquerque, New Mexico, (left) every driver has his own small screen and, on a good night, the drive-in movie circles handle 250 twentieth century wagons.

Some people go in for machines—for most of them
the greatest fun of all is to rev up the motor and take off.
They get a kick out of making a lot of noise, and the faster
they go the better they like it. For people who are addicted
to golf, however, wheels are simply a good way to get around
eighteen holes at a fast clip—so they can get around again
for an extra nine before dark.

Teenage hot rodder in Wyoming uses a motorcycle, the one in Maine takes off in a snowmobile.
Golf carts set a more sedate pace for the older generation.

Dune buggies, this one in Nevada, are a recent fad.

Pack trip in the Gros Ventre mountains of Wyoming

An autumn stroll among the maples of New England

Lone fisherman at Rialto Beach, Olympic National Park, Washington

Getting away from it all
is a treat for people whose working
lives are spent in the nerve-racking
atmosphere of our teeming cities.
Open country seems strange and
somewhat frightening to some, but
others find peace in the quiet beauty
of nature. They are happiest when
they leave their machines—and the
crowds—behind. They enjoy being
alone and on their own.

Paddle power in the canoe country of Minnesota

127

Boating enthusiasts—their number
is estimated at about 44 million—have
some 8.8 million pleasure craft at their
disposal. Estimates indicate that there
are about 620,000 sailboats, about 6
million power boats, and more than
2.4 million rowboats and canoes.
In addition, there are about 14,000
houseboats for people who like the
water so much they want to live on
it for at least part of the year.

Speedboat streaks across Long Island's Great South Bay.

Sailboats in a light breeze off Martha's Vineyard, Massachusetts

Yachts race on a close reach on Lake Pontchartrain, New Orleans

Neighbors and friends get together often in the cities and towns of America. They dance the old dances, play a hand or two of poker, and sometimes there's even a quilting bee—though there aren't many left who still know how it's done. In the old days, the ladies passed the time of day with a little gossip. Today the young people get together for what they call a rap session. It all adds up to just about the same thing.

Saturday night at the Legion Hall in Sauk Centre, Minnesota

Luncheonette in Madison, Wisconsin

The latest news in Iowa

A quilting bee in Missouri

A poker game in Minnesota

Weekend chores are always there
to be done. Children from half the
neighborhood come over for a barbecue,
and the young lady of the house gets
balky for no reason at all. There are
lawns to be mowed and leaves to be raked.
Out back somewhere there's a car to be
washed. Screens have to go up in the spring,
and someone has to take them down
again in the fall. It's the price we pay
for being a nation of homeowners.

There are 8.45 million girls in the
United States who are twenty to twenty-five years
of age. Using the ''cohort-component technique'', the Bureau
of the Census estimates that, by 1990, their numbers will
not increase beyond a maximum of 9.06 million. Considering
the evidence presented on these pages, the rate of increase
might be described as extremely disappointing.

There are daredevils who will try almost anything
—and call it fun. Sometimes they make it, and sometimes they
don't. The Hawaiian surfer below has everything under control,
but there are "wipe outs" in progress among those at right.
The mountain climber hanging out over an abyss at Yosemite can't
afford to make a mistake—and he doesn't make one. Skydivers
often try impossible stunts. This one is considered a "failure"
because *only* 16 of 20 jumpers actually got into the circle.

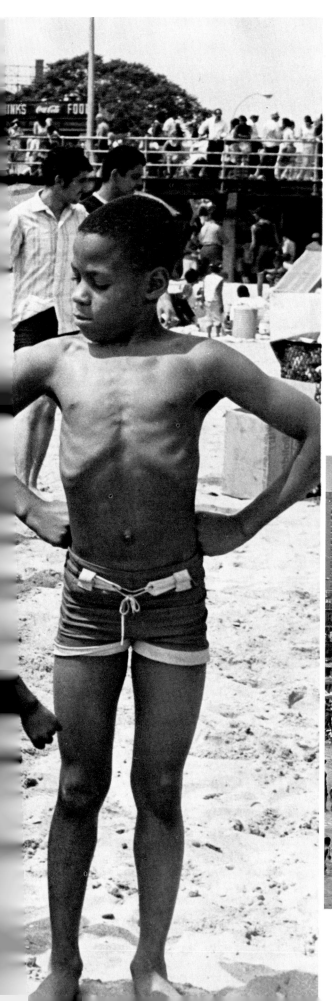

The muscle men on the beach at Coney Island, just a subway ride from New York City, aren't so very different from those who work out on Muscle Beach near Los Angeles. They're just a bit smaller, that's all. And the girls in their crowd are much less appreciative, because they're not old enough yet to know that they should at least *appear* to be impressed.

Winter sports can be as inexpensive
as coasting down the gentle hills of a
New England farm or the steep, short
runs in a city park. Or they can be
expensive, for those who seek the deep
powder of the Rockies and who will pay
the fee for a chair-lift to the summit.
It doesn't really matter, either way,
if skies are bright, the air is clear,
and there's fresh snow on the ground.

When the Pittsburgh Pirates won the Series in 1971 for the fourth time in 68 years, they hit front pages all over the country —and kicked off what local officials insist was *not* a riot back home. Ours is sometimes described as a nation in crisis, but nobody really worries about things like that when a ball team—playing almost *any* kind of ball—comes up from behind to make a big win. Baseball, football, and basketball are the great spectator sports in America. Almost everyone in the country either buys himself a ticket or watches the big games on television. And when the pros aren't doing very much, there's usually a game going on at the local high school or a nearby college.

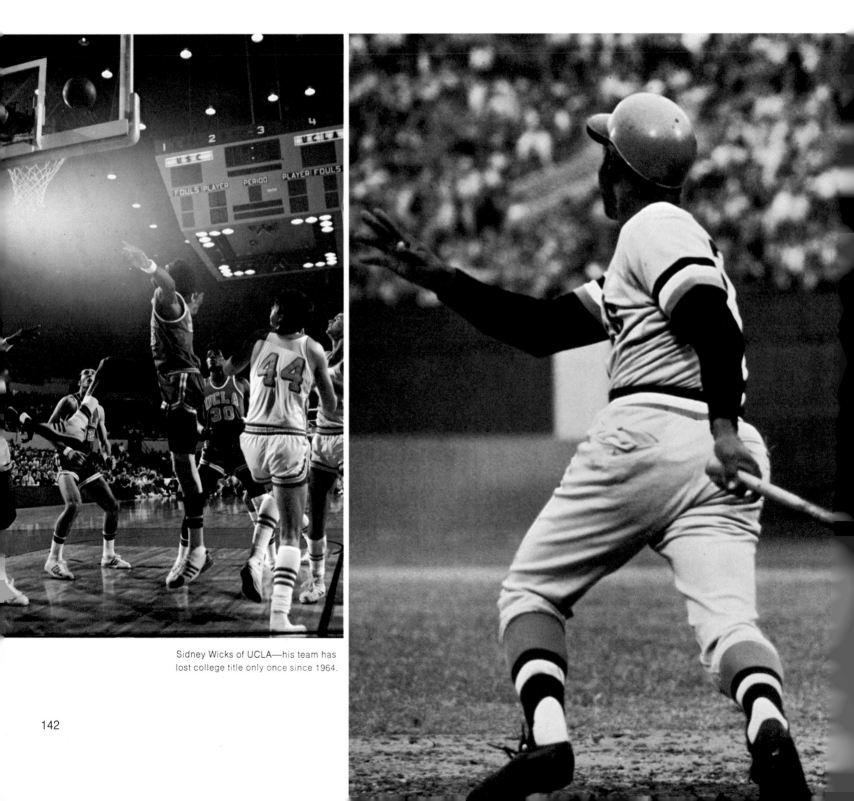

Sidney Wicks of UCLA—his team has lost college title only once since 1964.

Bruce Kison, 21-year-old Pirate,
pitches in first night game of Series history.

Dallas Cowboys beat Detroit Lions by 5-0 in the Cotton Bowl.

Roberto Clemente, left, hit .414 for the Pirates in World Series.

Summer vacations for Americans usually involve the family car. About 160 million people take vacation trips every year, and most travel a distance of less than 200 miles. They go to see the redwoods and Niagara Falls, or visit parks like Yellowstone and Yosemite. And wherever they travel, they take their cameras with them—to record their vacations for posterity.

Old Faithful Geyser, Yellowstone National Park, Wyoming

Redwood grove, Sequoia National Park, California

Yosemite National Park, California

Niagara Falls, New York

Scenic overlook in Tennessee

Sunday in the park is a way of life
for millions who live in the cities.
Here, in New York's great Central Park,
840 acres have been set aside for
recreation. Young lovers, entwined in
the branches of a tree, are oblivious to
the world around them; bicyclists stop
for animated conversation; a young couple
takes the baby for an outing. Elderly
ladies find companionship on a row of
park benches—on another, a young man
quietly strums his guitar.

A rocking chair and a game
of tag are proof that recreation
means different things at different
ages. The couple relaxing as the
evening light wanes are having a
wonderful time. They moved to Florida
after retirement, to settle in a
peaceful spot where the weather is balmy.
But to the youngsters racing along
below, there's nothing better than
playing tag. It begins with a
challenge: ''Hey hey, can't catch me!
'cause I run faster than a
bumble bee.''

Children know *how* to play—much
better than their more sophisticated elders.
The tiny girl on a chilly beach gets
sheer delight out of nothing more than
sea and sand—and a big brother to share
them with. Happiness, for the bespectacled
little girl pictured on the facing page,
is just wearing her brother's baseball
shirt and carrying his great big bat.
Statisticians tell us that more than 4
million men bought fishing poles in
1971. Did any of them have half the fun
of the kid who's just caught a
minnow-sized fish with a crooked stick?

150

4

The Arts in America

I t has been called a "cultural explosion," a "renaissance," and even "America's love affair with the arts." But whatever label is applied, a greater proportion of the American people today is involved, as audience or as creators, in more forms of cultural expression than at any time in the nation's history. Indeed, it is doubtful whether any people at any time has been so thoroughly exposed, so freely and amply committed, to so wide a variety of performing and visual arts, or has shown greater vigor and more ingenuity in shaping them to their own national experience.

There is little that is structured or academic about this phenomenon, although the schools are deeply involved and the critics spend much time and many words analyzing it. Rather, it is a free-swinging eruption that uses all the classic media of cultural expression and all the aids modern technology can supply, separately or in astonishing and exciting mixes. It draws on the treasures of the past accumulated in libraries and museums, on the experiences of the many races that comprise America, on the many problems confronting the land and its people, and the promises held out for both. It is essentially neither snobbish nor cultist (although there are plenty of snobs and cults), using the mass media and the chamber concert alike; rock and Bach, LeRoi Jones and Shakespeare, Norman Rockwell and Andy Warhol, the massive cultural center and the East Village loft. It is decentralized—New York, for all its size and cultural vitality, cannot approach the artistic domination of America that London and Paris exert upon their countries.

The thrust of the cultural explosion is youthful, and it is breaking down the old barriers between the "hearties" and the "esthetes" that

Johnny Cash, king of country music, comes from the rural South.

"The Band" plays country rock with skill and sophistication.

once divided college campuses. A high school student in California, for example, sees no inconsistency in being as proud of hearing his poetry read on the radio as in hiking fifty miles through the mountains; of playing a good clarinet and a good game of tennis; of working in the sun at an archaeological dig and in the darkroom developing his photos. Speaking of the young, author Kurt Vonnegut Jr. remarked in a recent interview: "They're the only people who read *anything* anymore. If they don't discover you, nobody will." Vonnegut is one of those youth has discovered; his hard-driving works fill the same role for the young generation that the cool bafflement of J. D. Salinger's "Catcher in the Rye" did in the 1950s.

It is the young who make rock music—including its offshoots, country rock and soul rock—and who gather in great hordes, as at the Woodstock Festival in the Catskills of New York, or in little groups around a recorder, a television set or a radio to listen. And rock, like jazz before it, is moving out of the arena of entertainment into fields formerly pre-empted by older forms: providing music for stage and church.

And it is the young who work in experimental theater and dance groups, who test new forms and colors with paints, who use everything— clay and plaster, tin and steel, stone and plastic—to shape the new sculpture.

The cultural explosion embraces all races, but does not homogenize them. Rather, Indians are looking to their own past for the color and form and sound that will reinforce their identity in this world they never made, encouraged by centers such as that in Taos, New Mexico. Black theater, soul rock, novels like Ralph Ellison's "Invisible Man" and James Baldwin's "Go Tell It On the Mountain" are among the forms and personalities that are transmuting the black experience into art. Black actors—James Earl Jones of "The Great White Hope," Sidney Poitier of many moving pictures—are among a large number who have distinguished themselves in recent years. Black singers like Leontyne Price have triumphantly traversed the long road from a rural ghetto to the applause of the opera world. Black dancers like Arthur Mitchell—performer, choreographer, and teacher—make their own special contributions to the range and intensity of the cultural explosion.

East Indian music followed the mysticism of the Orient into the American cultural scene, and the sitar joined the guitar as typical musical instruments of the day, just as the ukulele (from Portugal by way of Hawaii) and the saxophone typified the 1920s.

Not all Americans approve of the forms the cultural explosion has been taking—or of the hairy, uninhibited exponents of it. Some, like critic Jeffrey St. John, speak of "incoherent canvases, depraved plots in novels, tortured characters on stage and screen, and the anguished, ear-puncturing music." Mr. St. John approves the popularity of such moving pictures as "Love Story" and "Patton" as signs of a welcome nostalgia. But the sentimental and the classic have never been absent from our culture. Classical music was never more popular and available, and a Rembrandt can bring more people to a museum than a Warhol. Norman Rockwell's large and expensive volume of fine anecdotal paintings sold very well, and the modern realism of pop art would find it hard to hold its own in a contest with the classic realism of Andrew Wyeth. The cultural explosion is encompassing enough for all.

Out of its ferment, moreover, have emerged works and artists that have won international attention and the recognition of the critical elite. For more than a quarter of a century, the most innovative and influential painters have not been found in Paris. They have emerged from the American school of Abstract Impressionism—Jackson Pollock, Franz Kline, and Adolph Gottlieb among its leaders; from the popular, or "pop" art of Andy Warhol, Jasper Johns, Robert Rauschenberg, and others; or from the "op," or optical art that capitalizes on the eye's own illusions, as exemplified by the work of Morris Louis, Larry Poons, and Ellsworth Kelly. In sculpture, too, David Smith (whose technical background is automobile welding) is noted for his application of steel and bronze to inspired geometric forms, and there are many others, Donald Judd and Robert Morris among them, who are winning acclaim in this particular field of art.

In the dance America is taking over the pre-eminent position once held by the Russians. The pioneering work of Isadora Duncan and Martha Graham is being carried on by such free-wheeling experimenters as Merce Cunningham and Alvin Ailey. The classic disciplines imposed by George Balanchine have been among the influences creating great ballet companies, including Balanchine's own New York City Ballet. The influence of American dance is strong in many European companies, and Benjamin Harkavy, of the Netherlands Ballet, has said that "American dance is the most advanced and richest in choreographic development in the world today."

In architecture, it was the American mastery of the application of steel and glass to soaring constructions that first captured world imagination. Then Frank Lloyd Wright provided leadership in adapting buildings to American space and environment; later Eero Saarinen, I.M. Pei, Edward Durrell Stone, and John Carl Warnecke expanded on his tradition. Even more influential may be that Renaissance man, R. Buckminster Fuller, whose writings excite builders and planners while his geodesic dome has formed the basis of a widespread architectural trend.

In the novel and in play-writing, the products of the current American scene may not have as profound an impression as Nobel prize-

Alvin Ailey's American Dance Theatre

George Balanchine with
his New York City Ballet

winners Ernest Hemingway, William Faulkner, John Steinbeck, and Eugene O'Neill. But Norman Mailer, Saul Bellow, Truman Capote, Bernard Malamud, and many others attract respectful attention and translation abroad. The same is true of playwrights of the stature of Tennessee Williams, Arthur Miller, and Edward Albee. And poets as unlike as Robert Lowell and Allen Ginsburg are testing idioms suited to today, as T. S. Eliot, Ezra Pound, and Walt Whitman did in their eras.

In music, the recent death of the Russian-born, naturalized American, Igor Stravinsky, called attention to the fact that his polytonality was an extension of the mode in which Charles E. Ives—part insurance man, part composer—pioneered at the turn of the century. There are American composers like John Cage, who experiment with "mixed media"—sight and sound. And others, like Milton Byron Babbitt and Walter Carlos are exploring the dimensions that technology can add to music, using "instruments" like the electronic music synthesizer. In less radical forms, Samuel Barber, Virgil Thomson, Walter Piston, Aaron Copland, and the transplanted Italian, Gian Carlo Menotti, stand out.

Walter Carlos, who created "Switched-on Bach" with an electronic music synthesizer

And there are composer-conductors of the versatility of Leonard Bernstein, performers on the violin like Yehudi Menuhin, and Van Cliburn on the piano. There are orchestras—great orchestras—in Philadelphia, New York, and many other cities. The Metropolitan Opera Association of New York rivals the best in the world.

The lively arts, too, the truly popular arts, attain their own high levels in the cultural explosion. Musical theater has been an American speciality for a half-century. Men like George and Ira Gershwin, Cole Porter, Richard Rodgers, Oscar Hammerstein, Moss Hart, Alan J. Lerner, Frederick Loewe, Jerome Kern, and Irving Berlin created a musical idiom that has given years of pleasure to theater-goers. This great tradition is maintained today in such diverse hits as "1776," based on the founding of the nation; and "Hair," whose youthful road companies have packed theaters throughout the United States as well as in London, Paris, Tokyo, and other foreign cities.

Nor has Hollywood failed to make its impact. The western is imitated by many foreign film-makers; the regular product of the American studios remains a staple of world entertainment. Though critics have sneered, "Love Story" has been enjoyed by millions of Americans. In London, the influential magazine *Punch* told its readers that it was admirably done: "Don't be misled by all the talk: it could be very sentimental, but it is *not* sentimentalized."

And if, in general, movies no longer offer Americans the thoroughly good stories and light musical comedies they once did, it is due to

the impact of that most popular of inventions—the television set which is

John Wayne, king of the westerns

Conductor-composer Leonard Bernstein

The rock music hit, "Hair"

159

found in virtually every home. American productions are shown on small screens around the world (there was something of a public furor when "Peyton Place" was moved from one time-spot to another in New Zealand a few years ago). "Sesame Street," that striking American innovation in preschool education, is being adapted for use in developing countries by the United Nations Educational, Scientific and Cultural Organization.

These are only a few examples of the vitality and diversity of the arts in America. What is even more impressive is the number of people in our country who actively *participate* in the arts. There were more than 700 million admissions to our 5,900 museums in 1970—almost five times as many as in 1955. And the museums are reaching out to ever wider publics with neighborhood showings of loan collections, traveling art shows, and concerts. To cite only one, the Michigan Council for the Arts, using a special train of converted railway cars, has moved exhibits and held art workshops from one end of the state to the other.

There are at least 6,000 amateur theater groups in the United States; more than 1,100 symphony orchestras; and about 650 groups presenting opera. Then there are the cultural centers. The newest of the major ones is the Kennedy Center for the Performing Arts, which opened in Washington, D.C. in September of 1971. Others range in size from Lincoln Center—covering fourteen acres in the heart of New York City, with an opera house, a concert hall, and two theaters as well as a library-museum and school of music—to the center in Brownwood, Texas, with an arena seating 4,500 and a theatre accommodating 1,600 on its two acres. These are of relatively recent growth, but they have spread from New York to Honolulu—and to towns of every size in between. They are examples of civic pride and, consciously, stimulants to commerce. A large number include sports arenas and facilities for conventions with their theaters and concert halls. But above all, they illustrate an increasing awareness throughout America that cultural activities are an important part of the civic scene.

Naturally, there are wide divergences in the size and resources of the groups and institutions included in these impressive statistics. A museum may be the Metropolitan in New York, largest in the western hemisphere, celebrating its centennial by displaying the treasures of fifty centuries. Or it may be the exquisite Phillips Collection, also celebrating an anniversary in Washington, D.C., the fiftieth year since Duncan Phillips opened his home and the art it housed to the public. Cezanne was featured in this exhibition, and the visitors who filed in, so many of them young, went as if guests at an informal gathering—not with the self-conscious air of "culture vultures" on the prowl.

There are theater groups working from the well equipped stage

160

Leonardo da Vinci's paintings attract crowds to Washington's National Gallery (right) and to New York's Metropolitan Museum (below).

Cezanne exhibit celebrates 50th anniversary of Washington's exquisite Phillips Collection.

of a cultural center, and others—like Boston's Charles Playhouse—from the stage of a former night club. The Actors' Theatre, of Louisville, Kentucky, is housed in a remodeled railroad station. The symphony orchestra may be the Philadelphia Orchestra, of world reputation, or a group of ardent amateurs sometimes aided by a few professionals. The dance may be represented by the celebrated American Ballet Theatre, or by a single dancer (with her husband acting as stage and music director) giving performances and lessons in tiny Death Valley Center, Death Valley Junction, California, (pop. 30).

Libraries range from the Library of Congress, with 60 million items in its collections—including books, manuscripts, music, recordings, motion picture reels, and talking books for the blind—to the local grammar school with a few shelves of reference books. The public library system is unexcelled. In 1970, there were about 7,200 public libraries not connected with schools in the United States. College and university libraries numbered more than 2,000, and the libraries of schools at lower educational levels totalled about 120,000.

But regardless of size or degree of professionalism, these, the classic tools of culture, are within reach of every American. Children may hear the beauty of Greece explained while looking at the stately forms of Attic vases. High school students may learn something of classical music by playing the tuba in the school orchestra, and adults whose education stopped too soon can catch up by poring over books in the public library. The budding Bernhardt rehearses on the stage of her local little theater; the balletomane limbers up at the bar of the local ballet school.

Nor are the classic tools the only ones with which Americans can fashion the stuff of dreams and loveliness, of mirth and tragedy. Since the culture of the consumer in a democratic society knows no artificial barriers between what the intelligentsia recognize as art and what his or her own tastes require, popular arts play an important role in American life. Sometimes they are transmuted out of their original sphere, as when Duke Ellington takes his music into cathedrals with his sacred concerts. Cults grow up around moving pictures, and photography moves from the family snapshot to the work of an Alfred Stieglitz or an Ansel Adams. Television may commission a Menotti opera ("Amahl and the Night Visitors") or screen an adventure series—there is something here for everybody. Television, radio, moving pictures, the camera, the tape recorder, and the record player give richness and variety to the culture of 210 million Americans. All the ingredients derived from our multi-cultural heritage are available—a lively mixture for everyone to enjoy.

Thus today's cultural explosion is the product of many forces. Technology is part of it—an increasingly important part. The diverse

161

strains that make up the American are part of it—Europeans of all countries, Asians, Africans, Indians, Polynesians have contributed to it. The consumer society provides the leisure and the affluence, and makes available what people want, not what some higher power thinks they should get. The old American practice of free association is very strong in cultural fields. So is individual initiative. Philanthropy, too, has done much to spread the tools of culture; increased community responsibility in the area of the arts is also at work.

Needless to say, this combination of forces was long in the making. The first European settlers in the New World brought very little in the way of books, paintings or fine furniture from their homelands, and what they did bring gradually accumulated along the Atlantic coast. Those who struck out for the West tended to leave even these things behind. A log cabin in a clearing might boast a cherished book or two, a single piece of good furniture and a few silver spoons. A wealthy man, like Harmon Blennerhassett, the Irishman who became entangled in the plans of Aaron Burr, might build a palace in the wilderness, with frescoed ceilings, costly paintings, mirrors, and carpets. But for the overwhelming majority of the first generation on the frontier, stark dwellings, grinding work, and an almost complete lack of cultural amenities was the rule. Some of the elements of folk art were preserved, however. Ballads from the homeland were sung; there was dancing when a husking bee brought neighbors together; whittling and weaving produced simple but sturdy works of craftsmanship—just as long whaling voyages gave men the leisure to carve and etch bone and ivory in that "scrimshaw" which has been described as the only important indigenous folk art, except for that of the Indians, we have had in America.

In the seaports, where trade brought wealth and leisure, additional tools of classic culture soon began to appear. Books, at first, were rare and expensive. The earliest libraries in the United States were parish libraries started with books sent over in the 1690s by Reverend Thomas Bray and the British Society for the Propagation of the Gospel in Foreign Parts which he founded. Then men began to band together to purchase books; Benjamin Franklin called the Library Company of Philadelphia, which he founded in 1731, "the mother of all North American subscription libraries." Meanwhile, books were also needed by the universities budding in Cambridge and New Haven; in fact, books were the cornerstones of higher education. It is related of Yale, for example, that a group of clergymen gathered at the home of the Reverend Samuel Russel in Branford, Connecticut, in October of 1701, bearing books "for the founding of a College in this Colony."

There were painters, too, in colonial America, whose primitive virtues are better esteemed today than in the recent past. The stage was sparsely represented—the first professionally produced play by an American, Royall Tyler's "The Contrast," was not written until 1786. Music was mostly choral. William Billings, the tanner who wrote music that was sung and played by Washington's army, was chiefly interested in hymnology. But craftsmanship flourished—fine colonial furniture is still cherished today, and Paul Revere is almost as well known for his silverware as for his ride. Domestic architecture, too, was taking on a beauty that was to flower during the federal period.

But these were grace notes of an essentially utilitarian approach to life. John Adams was well aware both of the limitations imposed by the strenuous conditions of life in young America and of the promise of the future. "My duty," he wrote to his wife in 1780, "is to study politics and war that my sons may have the liberty to study mathematics and science. My sons ought to study geography, navigation, commerce, and agriculture in order to give their children a right to study philosophy, painting, poetry, music, architecture, sculpture, tapestry, and porcelain."

In other words, the finest esthetic expression in the new land was probably embodied in such documents as the Declaration of Independence and the Federalist papers. A little later it might be the beauty—practical but still magnificent—of the clipper ship.

As the American dream began to be realized in increased prosperity, the nonutilitarian aspects of art began to find greater scope. In one community after another, a public school system was established, and town libraries followed soon afterwards. But it was not until 1800, when the federal government moved from Philadelphia to Washington, that the first great American library was founded. Initially, $5,000 was appropriated for the Library of Congress, which by 1814 possessed 3,000 volumes. These were lost when the British burned Washington in that year, but the purchase of Thomas Jefferson's excellent 6,487-book private library revived the collection. By 1850, the total was 55,000 volumes, and an enlightened Congressional policy would ensure the growth of the institution to its present eminence and utility. Free public libraries were stimulated by Andrew Carnegie, one of the first wealthy men in America to state, and practice, a system of philanthropy as a form of trusteeship. His words and his example were to bulk large on the whole American scene; he gave $60 million for some 3,000 free libraries, and the total of his benefactions was ten times that amount.

In other branches of classic culture, the nineteenth century was essentially a period of accumulation. This does not mean the America of the 1800s was creatively sterile. American writers—Washington Irving, James Fenimore Cooper, Nathaniel Hawthorne, Herman Melville, Mark

163

The White House, Washington
Monument and Jefferson Memorial

Twain, Henry Wadsworth Longfellow, John Greenleaf Whittier, Edgar Allan Poe, Ralph Waldo Emerson, and Walt Whitman—were winning wide audiences and international respect. Composers like William Henry Fry, Louis Moreau Gottschalk, and Stephen Foster were making themselves heard (the latter two notable for their use of native folk airs). A succession of painters and sculptors—going back to Benjamin West, Charles Willson Peale, and Gilbert Stuart—left their marks in this period. And there was George Caleb Bingham, whose genre work gives such a fine flavor of his time; George Catlin, who helped preserve the Indian heritage; Albert Bierstadt, who immortalized the sights of the Old West; Thomas Eakins, Albert Pinkham Ryder, and James Abbott McNeill Whistler, who broke new ground in form and color. The sculptors included Thomas Crawford, Horatio Greenough, Hiram Powers, and somewhat later—Daniel Chester French, Augustus Saint-Gaudens, Gutzon Borglum, and many more.

Meanwhile, classical music was being performed by symphony orchestras. These were established as individual or associative enterprises by conductors—most of them German—and later endowed either by community action as in Philadelphia, or by the philanthropy of men like Henry Higginson, who founded the Boston Symphony and for years supported it almost singlehanded. Although these orchestras played American works and gave training to American performers and conductors, their chief effect was to expose Americans to the best of the classical works that were being produced in older countries abroad.

Industrial design belongs in any history of American art, and architecture—although older as a recognized art—has much in common with it. Indeed, the great principle enunciated and exemplified by Louis Sullivan—first of the true moderns in architecture—that "form follows function" is the basis for industrial art, stripped of extraneous ornamentation. Originally, Americans used the materials as well as the ideas of Europe in their architecture—superlatively well, in the cases of Thomas Jefferson and Charles Bulfinch. But then Peter Cooper rolled the first structural iron in 1854; William Le Baron Jenney used an iron and steel skeleton for tall buildings in Chicago; and Louis Sullivan, breaking with old designs, launched the world into the skyscraper age of steel and glass.

American museums, like so many of our cultural institutions, began as a kind of private enterprise. Charles Willson Peale set up Peale's Museum in Philadelphia before 1810. Then, after the Civil War, the need for larger displays of art troubled many wealthy citizens, and several genuine and noncommercial homes for the fine arts were opened, including New York's Metropolitan. Private collectors contributed works, and soon the public art museum was well established in the United States.

164

Johnson Wax research tower in Racine, Wisconsin

Lever building in New York

United Nations
headquarters in New York

To some, this time of collecting, or accumulating, was distasteful. Henry James—acutely conscious of his countrymen's preoccupation with buying and selling—wrote in 1876 that to the American "the world was a great bazaar, where one might stroll about and purchase handsome things." Apart from that, James believed, the American of his day regarded "an undue solicitude for culture" as "a sort of silly dawdling." However accurate Henry James may have been in his picture of some kinds of Americans, he did not foresee what results browsing through the global bazaar would produce, in accumulating a stock of beauty on which the future American would build. Nor did he appreciate the genuinely American folk arts that were taking shape on the frontier, on the plantations, along the railways and canals of his native land.

There were songs and stories emerging from the cotton fields— new rhythms and a way of seeing things that old Europe never knew. As cowboys gentled the herd down for the night they evolved their own balladry. The homesteader, the railroad hand, the worker on the "E-RI-E canal" sang songs and lived adventures that would be bred into the American cultural bone. The whaleman sang his chanties, and Herman Melville took the whaleship as the setting for the vast-ranging human tragedy, "Moby Dick." The trapper and the Mississippi raftsman told wildly humorous stories, and Samuel Clemens, writing as Mark Twain, fashioned them into an epic of the Mississippi River, "The Adventures of Huckleberry Finn." This is a book which has been translated into many languages and read around the world.

Similarly, jazz came out of what the blacks of the South "heard 'singing' in their minds"—African rhythms beating out the sadness and joy the slave distilled from his heritage and his lot. Jazz began to take shape in New Orleans, with its cosmopolitan way of life, and especially in that quarter called Storyville, set aside for legalized prostitution. When Storyville was forcibly made respectable in 1917, the early jazz musicians drifted up the Mississippi to the brassy speakeasies of prohibition Chicago, bringing their "good-time music" with them. Then they moved on to Harlem—and out into the world.

There are great names in the mainstream of jazz—from Louis Armstrong, Sidney Bechet, Jelly Roll Morton down through the big bands, and their leaders and performers, black and white, who made America listen: Duke Ellington, Benny Goodman, the Dorsey brothers, Count Basie, Dizzy Gillespie, Thelonious Monk. And jazz made its way into musical theater and the concert halls, through Paul Whiteman, George Gershwin, and others.

Quite apart from the personalities and talents involved, jazz was a truly folk art, whose effect was multiplied by technology—the phono-

166

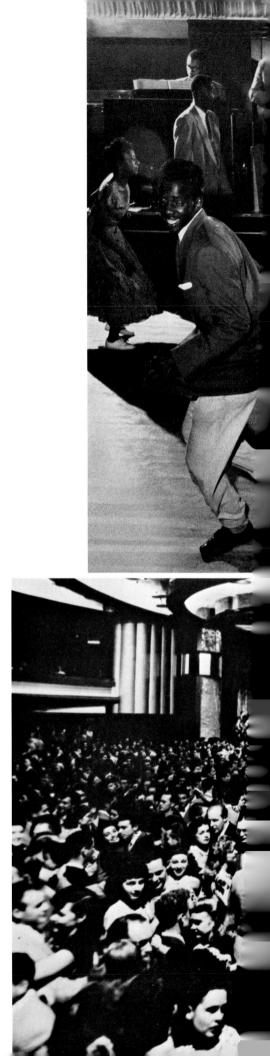

Stomping at the Savoy Ballroom in Harlem

Marching band in New Orleans, where American jazz was born

The big bands played the Hollywood Palladium in the 1940s.

graph and the radio. It was produced so widely because it satisfied popular taste. Like the westerns, public demand came first; recognition of intrinsic artistic potential followed—often reluctantly.

This aspect of the consumer culture has many manifestations. Basically, the comic strip is an ancient form which has been traced to the walls of Egyptian tombs. Its technique is used in the Bayeux Tapestry. In America, it was intended to help sell newspapers, and it still does so today. American cartoon strips were seen in 1967 by more than 200 million people in sixty countries every day. The comics were, and still are, sneered at by some. But they have produced such figures as George Herriman's Krazy Kat, Walt Kelly's Pogo, and Charles Schulz's Charlie Brown to intrigue the intelligentsia as well as amuse the world at large. They have inspired Walt Disney's animated film fantasies and affected the cinema and the stage in other, more subtle ways. In addition, they have given dimension to pop art (especially that of Roy Lichtenstein) as well as to graphics and decoration generally.

The present American cultural explosion thus draws its fuel from many sources. Basic are the folk arts—those that appeal to large numbers of people as enlightening, amusing, and stimulating. These the consumer society, aided by technology, provides.

Then there is the illumination shed upon these arts by the huge collection of treasures available in museums, libraries, and other classic repositories, such as the orchestra, the opera company, the ballet group, and the stage. Again, these are assisted by technology: television, radio, moving pictures, recording devices. Libraries, for example, are now called "resource centers" because their collections are not of books alone but of many other ways of recording the thoughts, sights, and sounds of different periods. The greatest and most varied collection in the United States, of course, is in the Library of Congress. Various forms of automation and computerization are making its resources, as well as those of other libraries, available in an ever wider geographical area. Many libraries are also reaching out to their communities. Orlando, Florida, offers a typical example: the public library there has a good collection of books, periodicals, paintings, tapes and records for loan, as well as a lively program of activities for children and adults—lectures, discussion groups, films, story hours, and plays. Moreover, like the museums, it has what Christopher Morley once described as "Parnassus on Wheels"— bookmobiles to broaden the reach of its branches in outlying areas.

Orlando, too, represents the increasing trend toward community and governmental participation in the arts, augmenting the still vigorous role played by philanthropy and by associations in this field. National participation in supporting the arts is relatively new; during the great de-

Main reading room at Library of Congress,
photographed with a "fish-eye" lens

pression, various federal programs for the relief of artists were launched, notably the Works Progress Administration's Federal Art Program. These, however, were emergency operations. President John F. Kennedy sought to place federal assistance to the arts on a more permanent basis. In 1963 he said: "I see little of more importance to the future of our country and our civilization than full recognition of the place of the artist. If art is to nourish the roots of our culture, society must set the artist free to follow his vision wherever it takes him."

Within the year, the young President was dead, but a fitting memorial to his devotion to the arts now adorns the shores of the Potomac. The John F. Kennedy Center for the Performing Arts was officially opened on September 8, 1971, with a stunning performance in the opera house of Leonard Bernstein's "Mass," composed especially for the occasion. In addition to the 2,300-seat opera house, the center has a concert hall which seats 2,600, and a theater (named for President Eisenhower) seating 1,100. The center cost $70 million, about half of it appropriated by Congress. Its 630-foot-long facade is sheathed in Carrara marble contributed by Italy. Other gifts from foreign countries include crystal chandeliers from Sweden, Austria, and Norway; tapestries and sculpture from France, Germany, and Great Britain; stage curtains from Canada and Japan. The total value of foreign gifts is well over $3 million.

In 1964, the year following President Kennedy's death, the National Council on the Arts was established, to become, in 1965, the advisory body for the National Endowment for the Arts. This latter agency has dispensed, since then, annual sums ranging from $2,534,000 in 1966 to $15,090,000 in fiscal 1971. Almost all funds were on a matching basis, some directly to individuals and groups, the rest to the states.

All fifty states, too, have arts commissions, and many cities have similar bodies which provide support to libraries, museums, theaters, opera, orchestras, and other cultural groups

This governmental interest in the arts is practically useful and esthetically significant because it shows that the American as taxpayer, as well as the American as ticket-buyer and donor, agrees with President Kennedy on the importance of culture to his life and future. Individual initiative, however, is still strong. The great new Los Angeles County Art Museum was launched in 1957 when Norton Simon offered matching funds to help the old museum build a new home. Money soon poured in in amounts ranging from Mr. Simon's own gifts—which, in addition to money, included a Rembrandt he had purchased for more than $2 million—to a flood of $10 gifts, which arrived for months at the rate of 200 a day. And then there was the case of the Kansas housewife who borrowed works of art from local museums, converted her station wagon

into an "artmobile," and toured the countryside for the benefit of those who could not easily reach a more static treasury of the arts.

Another source of artistic support is the great foundation, and a relatively new one is the corporation. Corporate sponsorship of artistic events on radio and television has become commonplace; a greeting card company funds distinguished plays on television; a petroleum company sponsors live radio broadcasts of the New York Metropolitan Opera. And this is being extended; a steamship line subsidized a new production of the opera "Aida," and eighteen corporations combined to sponsor one of the Metropolitan Museum's hundredth anniversary exhibitions in New York. There are those concerned with the financial backing required by the arts who believe corporate support may become as important as that provided by individual donors or governments.

But it can never be forgotten that the consumer, the paying audi-

New opera, "Mass," by Leonard Bernstein, opened Kennedy Center in 1971.

John F. Kennedy Center for the Performing Arts,
Washington, D.C.

Sidewalk
exhibitions
are a summ
tradition.

Young cellist practices during Vermont's Marlboro Music Festival.

Sunday painter in Cincinnati, Ohio

Duet with flute and guitar in a city park .

ence, the person who chooses what he would like to see, hear or read, is fundamental to the arts in America, as to so many other aspects of this society. He is the one who creates the affluence and the leisure which permit the arts to flourish; who pays the taxes or buys the goods which allow governments and corporations to foster cultural activities; and who, in the last analysis, will determine what shall live and what waste away in the wide flowering of artistic expression in America.

For commercial discipline has never been as rigid as state discipline, and the mass audience is not as confining as the class audience. It is charged against the consumer approach, for example, that the search for profit and the desire to reach the largest possible audience reduces the quality of the product to some lowest common denominator. But it is clear that when the Broadway stage becomes too profit-minded, the innovator goes off Broadway, and if any New York production limits him, there are regional theaters, university theaters, and resident theater groups like Washington's Arena Stage and Houston's Alley Theater.

There is no one in America to impose, let us say, "socialist realism" on the arts; no group or government to set the standards, lay down the rules. This has not been true in other times and other lands. It is too often forgotten, for example, that while Molière—under royal patronage—was free to satirize bourgeois gentlemen, bluestockings, and medical men, he was not free to point up the stupidities of the court of Louis XIV. Even Shakespeare hewed quite closely to the nationalist and dynastic conceptions of the Elizabethan Age.

The cultural explosion leaves every American free to seek his own ways of art. With little regard for any esthetic theory, a great flood of entertainment, escape, and enlightenment flows over the American scene. The American traveler no longer has to buy sketches or engravings of the scenes he visits—he snaps them with his camera, and takes, however humbly, a part in that art of capturing truth with light which is so basic to so many modern arts. If he prefers, he can use his leisure and his money to engage in any number of handicrafts, from Sunday painting to making jewelry (materials and instruction are in full supply) and thus draw closer to the old ways of art. His work may eventually join the mainstream of high art, as did the sounds of Storyville; more likely it will give him a purely personal satisfaction. What he sees on the television screen may move him with a great emotional experience; more often it will afford a laugh or a moment of delight.

But the whole range of art—graphic, plastic or performing—is open to the American to participate in and enjoy: a world of culture is at his command. Whether it shapes his life or merely colors an idle hour is for him—not some government, class or clique—to decide.

In America the arts are for everyone

Ice cream is permitted at childrens' performances of Cincinnati's Summer Opera Company, which is quartered in a pavilion at the local zoo.

Music lovers bring picnics, blankets, and folding chairs to Columbia, Maryland, where they listen to a symphony orchestra.

Millions of people now share our cultural life as listeners and viewers, and as active participants. The arts are no longer the province of a wealthy elite, and their benefits are available in small towns as well as in great cities; in parks, theaters, and concert halls; on records and tapes; on radio and television. America has more than its share of talented professionals, but it is the spontaneous enthusiasm of amateurs in every state that gives our culture its tremendous vitality.

A home-style performance is taken as seriously by these members of the school orchestra of Irwin, Iowa, (below) as by the rehearsing musicians of the Southern Indiana Symphony Orchestra in New Albany, shown at left. The performance at New York's opulent Lincoln Center is certainly more professional, but the intermission audience could not possibly enjoy it more than the parents below are enjoying their own private concert.

Sheer delight is mirrored in the eyes of a two-year-old in Chapel Hill, North Carolina. He is taking his first lesson on a miniature violin. Children learn to love music at an early age when teachers make a game of learning clefs and notes, and when grade school orchestras are led by conductors who can inspire the intense concentration shown by the two boys pictured on the opposite page.

Ballerina Patricia McBride stars in Jerome Robbins' "Dances at a Gathering." Edward Villella soars through the air in "Prodigal Son."

Ballet students perform with 112-piece school symphony at Interlochen Arts Academy in Michigan.

Lyrical grace and controlled power are the hallmarks of the great professional dancers who electrify the stage of Balanchine's world-famous New York City Ballet. The years of training required to produce such stars as these begin in early childhood in America's outstanding ballet schools.

181

An overloaded brush makes the project more difficult, but the boy (right) works on his masterpiece with infinite care.

The chance to create and to express themselves fascinates most youngsters, and introduces them to the world of art. Free instruction is available to the children sprawled on the floor at the Cincinnati Art Museum, and the self-possessed young lady sketching in the garden of New York's Museum of Modern Art has a chance to practice what she's learned at school. There may be no Rembrandts here, but the art produced will be proudly hung— somewhere on the walls at home.

Sometimes more paint gets on the painter than on the painting, but this is half the fun for the preschool artist.

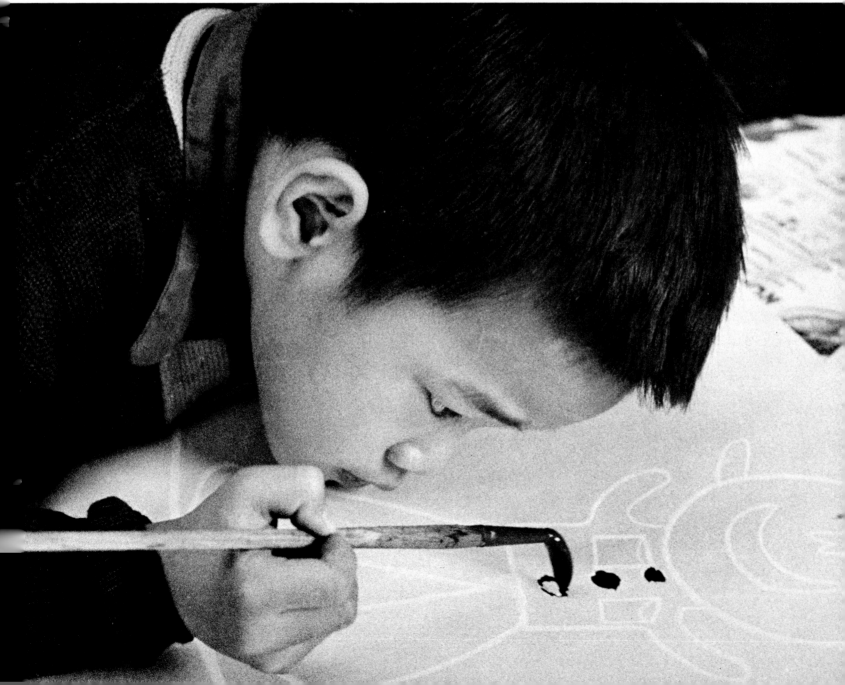

Modern architecture in America today is
as diverse as the talents of the great architects who
create it. The concept behind Frank Lloyd Wright's
controversial Guggenheim Museum in New York
is revolutionary for a building of this type. Totally
different in style, but equally revolutionary in concept,
is Eero Saarinen's magnificent Dulles International
Airport in Virginia (below). The deceptive and
elegant simplicity that makes New York's
Seagram building (at right) one of the greatest
skyscrapers ever built is the achievement of
Ludwig Mies van der Rohe.

Craftsman inks plate of five-foot-long Roy Lichtenstein lithograph. Below, sculptor Richard Serra works with molten lead.

Lynda Benglis, at right, creates a "floor piece" for the University of Rhode Island.

The **uninhibited vigor** of our younger artists—and their free-wheeling experiments with new forms, colors, and materials—are influencing artists all over the western world. Much of what they do may not stand the test of time, but their vitality and versatility promises to maintain for the U.S. its pre-eminent position in the field of modern art.

The Santa Fe Opera in New Mexico's capital city is one of about 650 opera companies that perform in cities across the nation. During rehearsals, the opera chorus—mostly young—gives it all they've got. After a performance of Mozart's "Magic Flute," the company takes curtain calls to the enthusiastic applause of an appreciative audience. Lead parts are sung by professionals, but the company encourages young talent and includes "apprentice artists" in its casts.

Earl Hines, pianist and band leader

Louis Armstrong, whose trumpet solos and gravel voice are known around the world, died in 1971.

The sheer exuberance of jazz, called "good-time music"
in its earliest stages, swept it across the country and over the world.
Military band instruments, abandoned at the end of the Civil War, were
picked up by freed slaves. Because they were basically a singing people,
they used unorthodox, self-taught methods to reproduce the sounds they
heard "singing" in their minds. Those dented horns became the shining
trumpets of jazz and—with the piano that found its place later—poured
out an improvised music that combined blues, spirituals, and ragtime
into a very special and peculiarly American art form.

Duke Ellington, fabled as composer,
bandleader and pianist.

Charlie Parker played bebop
in the 1940s, died in 1955.

191

Ornette Coleman made it big in the 1960s
with his unconventional saxaphone technique.

The religious heritage of our country can be read in the
beauty of its churches. The delicate spires that top the white
frame churches of New England remind us of the indomitable faith
of early settlers, who built lovingly with the simple materials at hand.
There are modern chapels, constructed of steel and glass to give color and
light to their soaring interior spaces. And there are great Gothic cathedrals
in our cities, rivalling those built by our ancestors in Europe, centuries
before western man knew this continent existed. Whatever their design,
these houses of worship are oases of peace in a troubled world.

The Air Force Academy Chapel in Colorado uses steel
tubing separated by shimmering panels of stained glass.

The National Cathedral in Washington was begun in 1907, will be completed in the 1980s. It serves all denominations, has been paid for—stone by stone—by individual contributions alone.

Country church in Lower Waterford, Vermont

Cleaning up oil spills in
San Francisco Bay (above and below),
and Tampa Bay (at right)

5

A Nation of Volunteers

They came together on the shores of San Francisco Bay, as they had done eleven months earlier in Tampa Bay, but this time there were so many volunteers it was hard to find constructive work for all to do. The first to show up were bearded, long-haired hippies. They had time to spare, having arrived before the sticky, viscous mess of oil began drifting back in on the tide. Twelve hours after two tankers had collided in the fog near Golden Gate Bridge, the cleanup was underway. The following day, January 19, 1971, thousands of other people took time off—businessmen, housewives and bus drivers, children released from school, and old people who wanted to do what they could. It was a filthy job and the water was cold, but no one complained. A high school girl with long, silky, blonde hair expressed the thoughts of many when she told the *National Geographic:* "How could we just sit there while the beaches got polluted, and the birds were dying? We wanted to *do* something. We wanted to get *involved!*"

This desire to volunteer, to take direct action as an individual—this sense of involvement—is a unique part of the American tradition. Almost a quarter of the American people—55 million—give time and effort to some 5 million voluntary associations. In 1970 they contributed more than $18 billion to various causes, and the value of their unpaid labor, at the lowest possible estimate, was another $14 billion in the same year!

These huge figures stand for many things. They show that Americans recognize, in John Donne's famous words, that "No man is an Island entire of itself," and with this recognition, each person is "involved in Mankind." More, the statistics demonstrate that in America such involvement need not be as a unit in a labor force, or as a political cipher. It can be a self-chosen, self-respecting, prideful engagement with others to attain goals that seem good and significant. Finally, this is a *workable* method, within a democratic framework, to attain such ends.

How well this method does work is borne out by the fact that in 1970 there were just thirty-two cases of paralytic poliomyelitis in the United States—two of them fatal. This is a very simple statistic. But to those who still remember the grim summer of 1916, when there were 27,363 reported polio victims in the country—9,023 in New York City alone—and more than 7,000 deaths, including 2,448 in the city, or to the much more numerous group that can recall the early 1950s, when the average annual number of cases paralytic polio was more than 18,000, it is a very dramatic figure.

Equally dramatic is the way this drastic reduction in a tragic incidence of disease was achieved. For the fight against polio has been justly called a "folk epic" in that it enlisted the emotions and the hard work of a great number of Americans in voluntary association to achieve a common goal. The March of Dimes, directed by the National Foundation for Infantile Paralysis, has been termed "the most intensive and comprehensive attack upon a single disease ever launched by a private agency anywhere in the world." It was in the authentic American tradition, a tradition as old as the Mayflower Compact, as effective as the Anti-Slavery Society, as "today" as the Friends of the Earth and the National Peace Action Coalition.

George Romney, Secretary of Housing and Urban Development, has said: "The best solution to the human problems of one individual often begins with the constructive involvement of another individual. Nothing can dissolve an individual human problem faster or more effectively than the willingness of one person to involve himself voluntarily, persistently, and sensitively in helping someone else to help himself."

And because of the scale on which such involvement takes place in the United States, it becomes a means for seeking the answer to national problems. It constitutes that "third force" (with government and business) that National Association of Manufacturers consultant Richard Cornuelle called for in 1965; that "third set of bridges" to a better life that President Nixon cited in his campaign; "the legions of the concerned and committed" to whom he appealed in his inaugural address.

Miracles were achieved through co-operative effort in the virtual social vacuum that existed in the early America, and along the frontier—where government was either nonexistent or severely restricted in the scope of its activity. Virtually everything, then, had to be done by groups of individuals working together—from common defense to the building of roads. But as the United States has grown more massive and more com-

Neighborhood boys' club in Atlanta, Georgia

Teenagers collect donations for March of Dimes.

plex, voluntary efforts have adapted to new and changing conditions.

Into the attack on polio, for example, went the individual will and determination of such men as Doctors Jonas Salk and Albert Sabin, the administrative talents of Basil O'Connor and John F. Enders, the efforts of publicists like Paul de Kruif, philanthropists such as John D. Rockefeller, Sr., and Jeremiah Milbank, Sr. Pharmaceutical firms aided in research and manufactured the vaccines, distributing them at cost during the first massive field test in 1954 when hundreds of thousands of children were vaccinated. Technology created the respirator, the "iron lung," and government at many levels set standards and organized care and treatment. But at the firm and essential base of the whole effort were those millions of ordinary people who gave, between 1938 and 1962, $630 million to the cause, in what one historian has called "an exhibition of almost religious fervor."

This phrase has a special accuracy because, in the religious heritage of America, the charitable impulse owes much to the Mosaic injunction to "open thine hand wide unto thy brother, to thy poor and to thy needy, in thy land." The continuing tradition of giving, of collaboration for worthy purposes, is represented today by America's 129 million church members and the organizations they support. That tradition was very strong in the lands from which most Americans came, where churches were closely linked to the existing order. But here the churches were fragmented among many sects and creeds. So, while there was and is a strong religious impulse behind works of charity and social use in America, there is far greater emphasis upon the individual conscience and on voluntary secular association.

Therefore, while most educational and philanthropic foundations in early America tended to be not only religious but sectarian, (names like Wesleyan University, Presbyterian Hospital, and a wide range of Roman Catholic institutions recall this fact) there were so many different faiths represented, and so much of the movement which created these institutions sprang from individual and voluntary group effort, that they tended toward the improvement of social conditions generally, rather than the spread of religiosity itself.

So, in association, Americans founded hospitals and experimented with improvements in prison systems. They organized to assist the needy with food, money, and—in the early days of the Association for Improving the Condition of the Poor—with free baths. Their missionaries in Oregon, in Hawaii, in India, and in China not only preached but gave medical care and started schools, taught new methods of agriculture, and developed alphabets for unwritten languages. The temperance movement, an early one in our history, grew into the politically powerful

197

Anti-Saloon League. Much later, useful and effective organizations like Alcoholics Anonymous were formed. In 1881, Clara Barton founded the American Red Cross, based on the work of the Swiss, Jean Henri Dunant; Jane Addams and Lillian Wald imported the British idea of the "settlement house" into Chicago's Hull House and New York's Henry Street Settlement, effective progenitors of a system of social work among the urban underprivileged that has become an honored profession today. And Lawrence F. Flick formed the Pennsylvania Society for the Prevention of Tuberculosis, germ of a national society, the first American association of lay and medical people devoted to the conquest of a specific disease, highly successful in its own field and an inspiration for dozens of its kind that were to follow.

This history of versatility in attacking so wide a range of objectives provides the basis for the American hope that volunteer effort, working with government and private enterprise, can be a major factor in attacking the whole spectrum of problems that concern us so deeply today. It explains why more and more established institutions depend on volunteer assistance, why the federal government itself has launched such voluntary groups as the Peace Corps, serving abroad, and its domestic affiliate, VISTA, serving among the poor at home.

And it also explains why President Nixon, after forming the Cabinet Committee on Voluntary Action "to maximize the degree of federal encouragement, assistance, and recognition of voluntary programs," on July 1, 1971, created ACTION, an agency to contain voluntary agencies directly sponsored by the government. These include—in addition to VISTA and the Peace Corps—Foster Grandparents and RSVP (Retired Senior Volunteer Program); SCORE (Service Corps of Retired Executives); ACE (Active Corps of Executives); as well as special volunteer programs within the Office of Economic Opportunity.

Government agencies have co-operated with the privately funded National Center for Voluntary Action, headed by Henry Ford II and Edwin D. Etherington. The two agencies work together to appraise, advise, and coordinate volunteer work to make it more effective—a necessary task in these days when the range of work is so broad and the context in which it operates is so complex.

For almost nothing—human, societal, environmental, or economic—is foreign to the volunteer. He may choose to get together with a few friends to clean up a neighborhood eyesore, or may instead join forces with millions who—assisted by government and industry—are attacking the root causes of problems which are national in scope.

Health is one of the oldest fields of American voluntary endeavor, and today that free involvement constitutes perhaps the largest social

Teacher Corps intern helps student in West Virginia elementary school.

Red Cross volunteers provide disaster relief when hurricanes strike, visit the sick in hospitals like this one in Thermopolis, Wyoming.

movement in the United States. It is estimated to have the "active loyalty"—meaning services as well as money contributions—of not less than 15 million Americans. The American Red Cross alone has 2.3 million volunteer workers, and annual expenditures of nearly $150 million. It is most dramatically known for its work in disasters, but, increasingly, the Red Cross is becoming involved in the more stubborn difficulties of those who dwell so precariously in the inner cities. The National Health Council now has seventy-four member groups, including such specialized health agencies as the Muscular Dystrophy Associations, the American Cancer Society, the Heart Association, and many others whose combined volunteer forces total more than 9 million.

These are impressive figures. But what makes them live is the volunteer who trundles a book cart through a hospital, or helps an aged woman write a letter to her family. Or there are specific tasks, like the effort of the Arizona Society for the Prevention of Blindness, which sent a team to a Supai Indian village to test the eyes of forty-eight boys and girls there, then trained a local team to carry on the work.

Government—federal, state, and local—has been playing an increasingly important role in health. The federal effort lies in research; in the control of epidemic diseases; in establishing and enforcing standards for drugs and other commodities or conditions affecting public health; in maintaining hospitals for specifically national purposes, such as veterans' care; in financing hospital construction; and, especially, in systems for payment of medical care for the aged. Congress has also authorized the federal government to pay a third of the cost of educating doctors, nurses, ophthalmologists, and other medical specialists—including teacher training, student expenses, and the construction of medical schools. States also build hospitals, enforce rules on hospital and medical practice, and sometimes have their own systems of payment for the medically indigent who cannot cope with the increasing cost of medical and hospital services. Many cities are also very active in these fields.

But the voluntary hospital, founded by private funds, operated on a nonprofit basis, and sustained at least in part by philanthropic gifts and services, is still the most important single resource for providing care to the sick. These hospitals are managed by volunteer boards, and a third of them have a director of volunteers to guide individuals who wish to help. In 1970, of the 7,123 hospitals in the United States, 2,665 were operated by federal, state, or local governments and 3,600 were voluntary nonprofit hospitals. In addition, there were 858 privately owned and operated "proprietary" hospitals, run on a profit basis.

The role of the voluntary hospital is even more important than its numbers suggest. Often associated with a school of medicine, it plays an important innovative part in dealing with health problems. Since, except in the maintenance of high standards of care and safety, it is less shackled by governmental restrictions, it has more latitude to work out methods that will improve administration. This is recognized by government: in New York City several voluntary and city hospitals are paired. Top administration and special medical skills are provided by the voluntary member of the team.

Poverty and its alleviation constitutes another of the traditional fields of voluntary endeavor in the United States. Participation of volunteers in the problems of the poor provides a powerful leaven of involvement, both for the helpers and for those who are helped, as well as the kind of experimentation that is easier for voluntary agencies than for government to attempt.

Prominent in the voluntary attack on poverty are such long established groups with religious affiliations as the Salvation Army, Catholic Charities, the various Protestant charities, and the United Jewish Appeal. Benevolent and fraternal groups, such as the Masons, Elks, Knights of Columbus, and many more have long given work and funds to the same general end, as have service clubs—Rotary and Lions International, veterans' organizations, Chambers of Commerce, and the like. The settlement house still flourishes in economically deprived areas—although the preferred name now is "neighborhood house"—often with help from local government in staffing and providing facilities.

But the increasing American concern over the urban aspects of the problem of poverty—the racial implications of the ghetto, housing, youth training, and the environment—has produced a number of specialized organizations and has given new directions to the work of the older institutions. Perhaps the most important of these new directions arises from the end of an old assumption that a soup kitchen or a handout constitutes the chief goal of charity. Now the emphasis, wherever possible, is upon the help that promotes self-help, and the assistance that enables a

Head Start volunteers (above and at right) work and play with underprivileged preschool children.

VISTA volunteer works on boat in Minnesota with Indian boy.

man, woman—or child—to acquire stature in his or her own eyes and take a responsible and meaningful place in society.

This is not easy when assistance and job training are provided under the mass of forms and formalities that government agencies almost inevitably entail, although the federal government has endeavored to humanize its own approach by such highly personal efforts as VISTA (Volunteers in Service to America), whose 4,000 workers operate in poverty areas. There is also Head Start, which seeks to give children whose environment may hamper their education the initial background required for effective public schooling. Head Start, Community Action—a program that covers a wider field in stimulating local action on local prob-

lems—and similar anti-poverty programs have about 600,000 volunteers.

Even these dedicated thousands, however, cannot resolve the basic problems of poverty. In 1971, 25.5 million Americans were classified as poor, with incomes below the government's poverty line of $3,972 for a nonfarm family of four. Again, as in health care, this area has seen an increasing assumption of responsibility by government. Federal, state, and local contributions to welfare in the fiscal year ending June 30, 1971, were $16.3 billion, nearly 27 percent more than in the preceding year. This outlay may appear high, but according to HEW, the fact of poverty is that 80.5 percent of the federally assisted welfare population—as of April, 1971—were aged, blind and disabled, or children under the age of sixteen. These 7.4 million children account for 55.5 percent of those receiving assistance. There were more than 2 million (15.6 percent) aged and more than 1.2 million (9.4 percent) blind and disabled. Only 126,000 able-bodied unemployed males were on welfare (less than 1 percent); 80 percent of these want work and about half are enrolled in work training programs. Of the 2.5 million (18.6 percent) mothers on welfare, 14 percent are working and 7 percent are in work training. Another 35 percent are estimated to be employable if they had day care centers for their children and job training for themselves.

The federal government has recognized the value of voluntary action in the area of welfare. This most massive and most controversial means of providing governmental assistance to the poor is in the process of major reconstruction. But one aspect of it—the bureaucratic machinery that the recipient must face—is being tempered by a new provision in the Social Security Act under which federal support is given to welfare programs. That support is now contingent upon the use of volunteers in carrying out this work.

Voluntary action may take many forms. In Los Angeles, more than 1,000 volunteers participated in a Share-a-Trip project, by which underprivileged children were given a trip each month to a zoo, a park, or some other place of interest and pleasure. One boy, whose capabilities had not previously been stimulated in school, was taken to an airport control tower by a former Air Force pilot. The experience stirred him; he made the school honor roll and is planning to go to college—while the ex-pilot has become a volunteer tutor.

Even more imaginative was the experiment in Lansing, Michigan, of pairing welfare families with volunteer middle income families. In one case, a young wife and mother, deserted by her husband, was helped to brush up on her education and to search for work—her children were looked after while she was absent. She won a Civil Service position and now heads a "pair family" herself with another welfare

Many cities have programs that encourage young people to clean up the litter in their own neighborhoods.

family. She said about the plan: "If it weren't for the volunteers, I'd still be sitting at home feeling helpless. I'm sure the workers were good, kind people but I was afraid of them; I relaxed with my volunteer family. I wasn't afraid to go out and look for a job because they knew where I was and what I was doing."

Much of present-day volunteer effort in both urban and rural regions is directed toward securing this type of response, toward inculcating a sense of personal worth and participation. A 1969 poll showed that 60 percent of all American adults—69 million—were willing to serve on local committees dealing with community problems, and that 13 percent had already done so. The range may be from local school boards—now being given increased authority in many areas to enhance the sense of neighborhood involvement—to block committees to speed up garbage collection and trash removal. PRIDE is an organization of ghetto youths that undertakes the latter task on a more or less permanent basis. Members clean up their neighborhoods and establish their own part in them at the same time.

And there is still room for the individual with an idea. In Hanover, Pennsylvania, Mrs. Sophie Leavitt was unhappy over the poor nutrition obtained by welfare families from surplus food allowances. She experimented, and developed simple recipes and menus from the allowance that provide adequate nutrition. She began giving demonstrations and cooking lessons wherever she could gather an audience of welfare clients. The response was so encouraging that the local TV station broadcast her lessons and menus. Eventually, the Department of Agriculture distributed them through a radio network.

Government and business have taken the lead in improving housing conditions for the poor—but the need is still great, and voluntary action supplements the work of the larger and richer organizations. Rehabilitation of decayed dwellings is sometimes undertaken on a block-by-block basis by those most vitally concerned. And in California's San Joaquin Valley, the Friends Service Committee helped organize Self-Help Enterprises, Incorporated—SHE. On its fifth corporate anniversary in 1970, it could point to more than 550 families who had built their own homes (quite literally, except for wall tiling, cabinet construction, and plumbing) under SHE's sponsorship and direction. Others were in process—enough to house, eventually, nearly 7,000 people, Chicanos, blacks, American Indians, Filipinos, and Anglos, alike only in needing good housing and having low incomes. The project is expanding, geographically and in other ways, and has the co-operation of both the community and the government, including housing loans and VISTA volunteers. More, it has a factory turning out ten prefabricated houses a month to supplement, if not eventually to supplant, the original barn-raising method of building which is today so costly in materials and labor.

These are some of the adventurous ways in which the old American tradition of voluntary association is being applied to the even older problems of poverty. But there is a darker side to the urban crisis than poor housing and malnutrition. Crime and its accomplice, the drug peddler, stalk the poor streets and ride the highways into more affluent areas. Drugs, in particular, know no class or income barriers. The simplest response, and one far from unknown in American history, is the vigilante organization, and patrols of streets and apartments have been organized by not a few groups. But since guards alone cannot cope with the problem, the volunteer reaction has been more sophisticated.

After all, the United States has a police force more than half a million strong, and pays about $4.5 billion a year to maintain it—a larger and better equipped force than the country has ever had before. But the corrosive resentment and fear that a rising crime rate inject into a community can have effects beyond the power of law enforcement agencies to cure, or prisons to quarantine. Admittedly, enforcement comes first, and that is primarily the task of the professionals. But to get at the roots of the problem, to prevent the criminal from emerging, to cure him of his addiction whether to crime, drugs, or both, to avert that danger against which the President's Commission on Law Enforcement warned—"The cost of the fear of crime to the social order may ultimately be even greater than its psychological or economic costs to the individual"—these are tasks in which voluntarism can play a major role.

To the extent that crime is spurred by poverty, everything the voluntary agencies are doing to combat that evil works against crime. In the same way, volunteer work in the field of education helps to combat juvenile delinquency by instilling self-respect and respect for others. Volunteers are also working in specific areas directly connected with the rehabilitation of offenders.

Since its inception in Illinois in 1899, there has developed in the United States a system of juvenile courts that has spread across the country. It stems from the idea that a young offender should be separated from older criminals even during the pre-trial period, and that he should be provided with special services to help prevent a first misstep from leading to a life permanently outside the law. But the courts have been swamped, the professional staff cannot cope, and the tendency of every institution to fall into rigid patterns has, in many cases, frustrated the high hopes held out for the juvenile court system. Yet volunteers were not welcomed until very recently. In May of 1967, according to Dr. Ivan Scheier, now director of the National Information Center on Volunteers

Veteran who became addicted to heroin in Vietnam has taken no more of it since he went on methadone maintenance program at a Veterans' Administration hospital.

in Courts, fewer than twenty juvenile courts in the entire country permitted volunteers to assist them.

Dr. Scheier, then a professor of psychology at the University of Colorado, was struck by the fact that Lee Harvey Oswald, President Kennedy's assassin, had been known to a juvenile court but had received little significant attention there. Dr. Scheier offered to supplement the probation staff of the juvenile court in Boulder, Colorado, with his own services and those of other concerned citizens. He eventually resigned his university post and developed a volunteer program for Boulder courts, wrote a manual for such programs, and provided consultation for other courts wishing similar services. Now he believes that nearly half the nation's juvenile courts are using about 150,000 volunteers.

In Denver, Colorado, a Partners Project has been established to work with juvenile delinquents. It operates on the assumption that a youngster who does not believe he has a future does not care if he has a past; that if he can develop a record of accomplishment which impresses his age group, he will gain self-confidence and self-reliance.

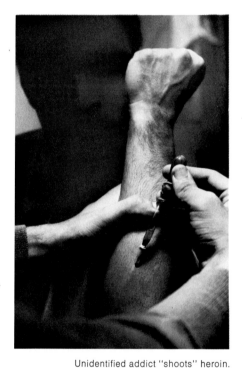

The project is wholly voluntary, for both partners. The senior is screened and given orientation; the youngster makes his own choice, with his parents' permission. The accomplishments may begin with a bobsled ride on a snow-capped mountain, or with successful fishing in a stocked lake. Cameras record the event—to build the ego and give substantiation and prestige among his friends. The senior partner visits the younger one's home and his schoolteacher, and the YMCA provides facilities for swimming, sparring, and craftsmanship. The plan has proved so outstandingly successful that many other cities have taken it up—even as far away as Juneau, Alaska.

Unidentified addict "shoots" heroin.
Marijuana smokers share a "joint."

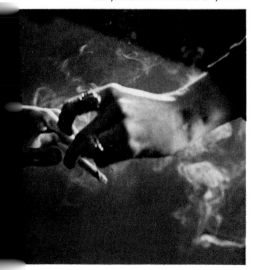

Besides the courts, volunteers are working in the crime-related area of drug addiction. Such voluntary agencies as Synanon and Phoenix House not only complement the work of government centers but also are sources of valuable information on approaches to this still thorny and little-understood field of therapy. And VISTO (Volunteers in Service to Offenders), composed largely of former addicts, is also helping narcotics users. It started in 1968 with 150 volunteers; by the end of 1970 there were nearly 1,000, and VISTO's fourteen area offices in Los Angeles County are state-supported.

The poisons men inject into their systems are matched by those that are unwittingly inhaled, or eaten. Pollution and the environment are big enough problems to require the concentrated efforts of government and industry, but the citizenry has its own responsibilities and its own means of combating such evils. Neighborhood groups gather waste materials for recycling; individuals are urged to co-operate, or to engage in similar activities on their own. Mrs. Adele Auchincloss, the wife of Louis Auchincloss, the novelist, organized an experiment on a two-family basis. One family continued in its usual way, serving as a "control." The Auchinclosses abandoned the use of paper towels, used net shopping bags, and refused all but essential wrapping, bought only returnable bottles and fresh, instead of packaged, vegetables. At the end of the week, with both families serving the same number of meals to the same number of persons, the control family had generated 107 pounds of garbage and trash to the 57 pounds of the Auchincloss family. The experiment convinced both families of the utility of the method.

There are broader efforts, of course. The work of such organizations as the Sierra Club and Friends of the Earth are directed at major threats to the environment. Some of the work of Ralph Nader and his supporters is also directed to this end. In the United States, such efforts take two broad forms: political, to influence legislation; and economic, to bring direct pressure on manufacturing and service industries. The American can play two major roles in shaping his country's destiny, as a voter and also as a consumer.

"Consumerism" is a word of many meanings today. It is applied, often pejoratively, to what critics consider a major flaw in the consumer society: the effort to induce more and more people to buy more and more goods. But it is also used for a movement in another direction: organized voluntary groups working through purchasers to raise levels of quality, to keep down excessive prices, to insure more accurate information about goods and services on the market, and to convince manufacturers and industry in general that the desire for reasonable prices, quality products, and an unpolluted environment are matters of common—and urgent —concern to a great many people.

In this sense, consumerism has obtained widespread governmental recognition. There are offices of consumer affairs under various names in federal, state, and local governments. At each level, laws and ordinances govern weights and measures, pricing methods, safety and health standards, and the like. Long established voluntary institutions, such as the Better Business Bureaus, aid in such efforts, and various nongovernmental research groups study and report on qualitative and cost differentials in merchandise.

In addition, there are many groups that have come together for specific purposes—such as the enactment of new legislation for consumer protection, or the enforcement of statutes already on the books. Such groups were largely responsible for passage of the "Truth in Packaging Act," to make shelf-selection less chancy in terms of price and quality; the Consumer Credit Protection Act (Truth in Lending), to make inter-

Ralph Nader, consumer advocate

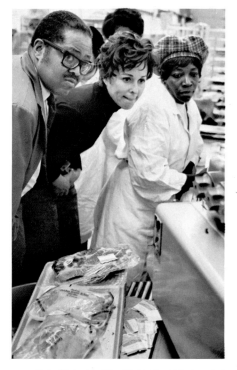

Bess Myerson, New York's Commissioner of Consumer Affairs, checks market scale.

Co-op grain elevator in Toulon, Kansas

COOP

est rates and the cost of credit purchases more understandable; the Toy Safety Act, governing the finishes and other properties of toys children are likely to handle carelessly; and amendments to update the Wholesome Meat Act of 1907.

As one effect of these efforts, a Bureau of Product Safety has been established within the federal government to implement the safeguards required by the Toy Safety Act, and the Food and Drug Administration has been sharply reminded of its responsibilities. For example, it is currently revising and tightening its list of food additives "Generally Regarded as Safe" (GRAS)—materials that can be incorporated into food products without notice on labels.

Thus, the enlightened consumer can join with his fellows to affect legislation. To provide enlightenment, such organizations as the AFL-CIO Department of Consumer Relations, with a largely volunteer work staff, gives courses to local union representatives, teaching them how to "deal with the market place" and helping their local members to be selective consumers. The Consumers Education & Protective Association, started five years ago in Philadelphia, now has eleven units across the country—groups of volunteers ready to investigate and to file complaints, and sometimes to back such complaints with demonstrations.

For the consumer groups have impact at point of sale, as well as in legislative halls. The Virginia Citizens Consumer Council, which claims to represent 70,000 Virginians statewide, began with a spontaneous "Ladycott," a refusal by a group of women in Springfield, Virginia to buy in local markets because of steadily mounting food prices. A year later, in 1967, the VCCC was incorporated—not to boycott but to advance the interests of the consumer in every area.

Co-operatives are an old and firmly established means of using voluntary methods to improve consumer or marketing conditions—as well as to achieve other ends. Farm co-operatives, for example, marketed more than a fourth of America's crops in 1970, and they maintain their own plants for processing foodstuffs. The consumer co-operative is a predominantly urban outgrowth of this movement. One, the Berkeley Co-operative of Richmond, California, owned by some 57,000 families in the Bay Area, has eight shopping centers and a sales volume of $40 million a year. It employs some 650 paid employees, but leadership is by volunteers, and much of the work (comparison shopping, for example) is done by volunteers. Co-op volunteers also man a collection depot for materials to be recycled, test recipes—its "Co-op Low Cost Cookbook" is in its seventh printing—promote interracial harmony among whites, blacks, and Chicanos, and press for consumer legislation.

Volunteer efforts in the field of legislation are by no means confined to specific consumer interests, or to those of the environment. The largest group of volunteers in America may well be the active members of political parties. This is sometimes forgotten in the stratification of the major parties and the indirect means usually used to select convention delegates and candidates. But one has only to glance at American political history to see, in such movements as those of the Populists of the Democratic Party and the Progressives of the Republican Party, how ground swells of opinion promoted by volunteers can crack the strongest of party structures. Even closer in time are such phenomena as the student volunteers who campaigned in 1968. Though they may have been unable to determine a presidential nominee, they nevertheless played a major role in deciding some of the primary contests. These were influential in causing Lyndon Baines Johnson, elected in 1964 by the largest plurality ever won by any American president (61 percent of the total votes cast), not to run again. They continued to be active, often with great effect, in the Congressional elections of 1970.

Outside the party system, the Chamber of Commerce offers courses in practical politics, with emphasis on local involvement. It boasts more than 1 million graduates in 1,800 communities who have attended the seven two-hour-weekly workshops that comprise the courses.

Older and even more influential is the League of Women Voters. It was founded in 1920, when the franchise was new for women in most states, to help them exercise that right intelligently and effectively. Now it provides not only objective and nonpartisan political information, but action as well—and not for women alone. The league—with a paid-up membership of 160,000—works at every political level on a varied program covering both domestic and foreign affairs. It played an extremely important role in the adoption of the Social Security Act of 1935; the Pure Food, Drug, and Cosmetic Act of 1938; the Water Resources Planning Act of 1965; the economic opportunity amendments to the Civil Rights Acts of 1967 and 1968; and many other key pieces of legislation. It has also been a staunch supporter of the United Nations since 1945, and lobbied in 1970 to defeat restrictive trade legislation. There are local leagues—1,300 of them—in every state, plus the District of Columbia, Puerto Rico, and the Virgin Islands.

A late and lively newcomer to the scene of voluntary political action is Common Cause, founded by John W. Gardner, former Secretary of Health, Education and Welfare. It started in September of 1970, with the announced aim of improving the quality of American life through extra-party political action, and in a little more than a year attracted a membership of 225,000. Its initial major effort was to attack the deeply entrenched and highly restrictive seniority system in the

208

Volunteers stuff envelopes during election campaign (above). Members of League of Women Voters (right) tabulate election returns in Arlington, Va.

Students ask Brooklyn, N.Y. shopper to support their Congressional candidate.

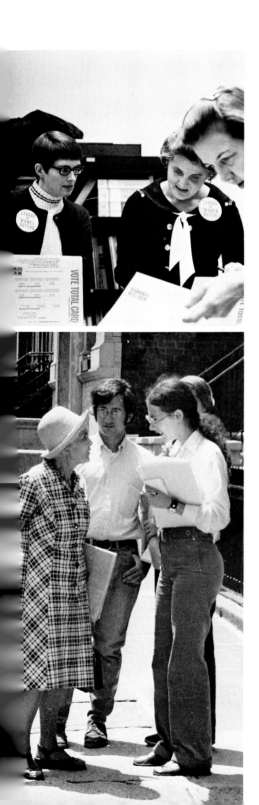

House and Senate. Progress is necessarily slow—but it is being made.

Whether the work of American volunteers is as broad in scope and goal as Common Cause or is one of those "small, splendid efforts" that Mr. Nixon called for at his inaugural—like Mrs. Leavitt's recipes—it has a three-fold effect. One is self-fulfillment for the volunteer; another is the satisfaction that comes from giving something of oneself to another; a third is the statement of a community of interest with one's fellow man, whether it be in a frontier husking bee, or in joining others to bring aid in some disaster many miles away. This is in the American style. In 1760, virtually all the colonies—then separated by distance, differences of cultures and economies, and even of language—hastened to send aid to Boston, ravaged by a great fire, just as today national resources are mustered for victims of an earthquake in Los Angeles, a forest fire in the Northwest, or a hurricane in Mississippi.

And this concern extends far beyond national boundaries. Today, when American ships and planes bring relief to sufferers from floods in Florence, a quake in Chile, a cyclone or civil strife in Pakistan, they are virtually taken for granted. For the United States long ago institutionalized such aid. In World War I, food supplies for German-occupied Belgium—and for the whole of a ravaged continent when the war had ended—made America a symbol of international generosity. And in World War II, between 1939 and the end of 1945, American citizens contributed more than $460 million in cash and kind for nonmilitary purposes abroad. For the United Nations Relief and Rehabilitation Administration (UNRRA), Congress appropriated $2.7 billion, or 73 percent of the money contributed by all governments, for its varied forms of assistance in the aftermath of war. Another $6 billion was given between 1946 and 1956 by individual Americans and voluntary agencies.

That this kind of aid, however philanthropic in motive, was also sound national policy is evidenced by the market America enjoys today in a prosperous Europe and in many other regions. The revival of Europe was stimulated by the Marshall Plan, whose purpose, in the words of George C. Marshall, was "to permit the emergence of political and social conditions in which free institutions can exist." Under the Marshall Plan the United States pumped $13.5 billion into sixteen European countries between 1948 and 1952. We now export—sell—more than that to Europe each year.

The Marshall Plan and other ventures in foreign aid have never been launched on the premise that they would bring a dollar-and-cents return on an "investment." Nor could they be considered—strictly—as volunteer efforts. But all such programs were paid for by the taxpayers, and none of them would have been possible if those taxpayers—through their elected representatives—had not approved the appropriations.

As in so many other instances in which massive problems are approached by massive injections of government funds, Americans have seen the wisdom of infusing humanity into foreign aid—personal service by volunteers. Such institutions as the American Red Cross and CARE involve individual donors and workers in projects that deal directly with people abroad, whether they are under the stress of some crisis—war, revolution or natural catastrophe—or simply struggling with the age-old problem of their environment. Similarly, the work of Dr. Norman E. Borlaug and other agronomists, whose miracle wheats were keystones in the "green revolution" that has transformed the world's food prospects, is carried abroad by many workers, government-sponsored or privately financed. And Dr. William B. Walsh's Project HOPE, begun in 1958, has trained more than 6,600 physicians, surgeons, nurses, and technicians in the special needs of the more than 3 million Asians, Africans, and Latin Americans to whom they have brought immunization, examinations, surgery, and other services on the good ship *SS Hope*. All the *Hope* medical crew are volunteers, many serving without pay.

The government has recognized the value of this kind of voluntary and personal involvement through the Peace Corps, which currently has 6,600 Americans of all ages and skills serving abroad. They are working closely with people to whom American aid might otherwise mean only a label on a box—something that some distant person or institution had bought and shipped. A good thing, no doubt, but only a *thing*. The Peace Corps volunteer, however, is a friend who helps—face to face.

The desire to *do* something, to become *personally* involved, is very deeply ingrained in the American character. We are not, and have never been, an indifferent or a passive people. At heart most of us are activists. Once we become convinced that a problem must be solved, we join together with others who favor our particular solution and do what we can to convince the rest of the country that our view should prevail.

"Relatively small groups of idealistic citizens," John Gardner has written, "won the vote for women, abolished child labor, launched the conservation movement, made family planning a respectable issue, forced us to care about retarded children, prohibited cruelty to animals, etc. Those who don't grasp the impact of such citizen action don't understand the workings of this free society."

This is the chief source of America's pride and hope, in a day when numbers grow larger and larger, institutions and problems growing with them. This is the vitality that sometimes results in confusion but offers the individual his leverage to move the world. This is the America that gives of itself—ever changing, ever renewing—to shape a better life for all.

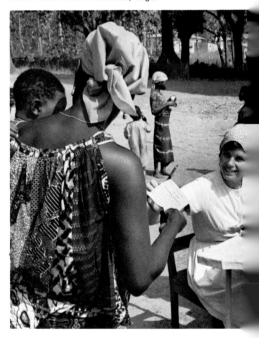

Peace Corps volunteer from Iowa helps local farmer build a wall in St. Lucia, in the Caribbean. Below, Peace Corps volunteer nurse from Ohio works with local assistant at infant care clinic in Sokode, Togo.

Korean child takes home a
basic CARE food package.

Sacks of flour (above) are distributed to the poorest segment of the population in India.

Campaign for the 1970s – to clean up the environment

The quality of our environment is a major concern to everyone who can see, smell or hear the world around him. Production has risen by a fantastic 138 percent in the last 25 years, and levels of pollution have risen simultaneously. We began to understand the problem in the 1960s, now we are doing something about it. The campaign for the 1970s is well under way, and *everyone* has a chance to participate—individually or as a member of an environmental action group.

Helping out at solid waste recycling station in Washington, D.C.

Sweeping the streets of
New York—on roller skates

Raising anti-litter flag on mountain
of trash collected in Dallas, Texas

213

Ecology group protests plan to run
overhead power lines through California park.

Unsightly poles and litter spoil view
of Statue of Liberty from Jersey City, N.J.

"We will bury you" is the slogan that best summarizes the sentiments of volunteers who object to the esthetic pollution of utility poles. Underground installation is safer, and is mandatory in more and more new subdivisions. After eight years of experience, the utility in Salem, Oregon, reported that decreased maintenance costs offset increased installation costs.

Utilities go underground: before and after conversion in residential Seattle, Wash.

Imagination and determination can work wonders in low-income neighborhoods. From Los Angeles to New York, young artists—occasionally helped by sign painters—are enlivening the bleak walls of factories and tenements. At right is a magnolia tree which was threatened by an urban renewal program.

Posing proudly in front of it are the determined grandmother and neighborhood children who raised $7,000 in a raffle to save the tree. The city finally saw the light, designated Brooklyn's own magnolia as a "living historical landmark," and will see that it is protected.

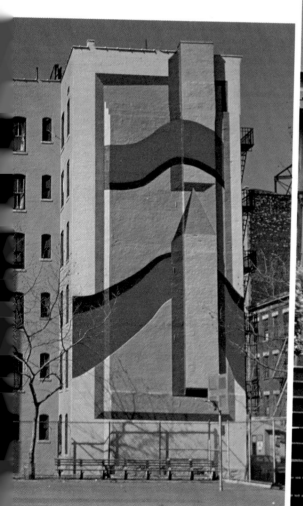

Air pollution is the target of citizen groups who have pressured government and industry into adopting new air-quality standards. Auto manufacturers are working hard to develop pollution-free engines, technicians are trying to reduce jet engine emissions and noise. The air we breathe is a national resource like any other, and most of us now believe that no one has the right heedlessly to pollute it.

Air pollution information is distributed in New York City, whose skyscrapers (right) can barely be seen through the smog.

TAKE CARE OF OUR AIR

environment!

University of Hawaii students wear gas masks during Honolulu City Council meeting to dramatize deterioration of air quality.

Water pollution is a challenge to volunteers, who sometimes take direct action by going out themselves to clean up the mess that has been dumped into local rivers and lakes. Other activists press for more effective sewage disposal systems, and for stringent regulations to control industrial wastes.

Sixty truckloads of debris were pulled out of New Jersey's Hackensack River by more than 1,000 volunteers.

Volunteer monitors water quality
by taking and testing water samples.

Industry and consumers must share the
cost of reducing industrial pollution; government
must set and enforce strict and uniform standards.
There are no real breakthroughs so far,
but technicians are working hard to find new
ways of reducing and recycling wastes.

Belching smokestacks near Detroit fill the air with iron-ore dust.

Twentieth century view of Mt. Shasta in California

Collagen, a water-soluble protein, may one day replace plastic food bags, plates, forks, spoons—even bottles.

Hydraulic press in Cleveland compacts garbage.

It's a tight squeeze for Virginia salesman, Pat Sappo.
It is sometimes possible to get a car into a parking lot like the one
shown at right, but the problem of getting the driver out of the car can be
almost insurmountable. He must have the determination of a linebacker and
the agility of a contortionist. Citizen groups in most urban areas have worked
hard, and often successfully, to put downtown parking underground.

Nearly 100 million cars—most of them
jammed into 2 percent of the land area of
the U.S.—clog the nation's roads today. The
patience of Job is required of commuters
who, five days a week, must ease their
cars off multi-lane superhighways onto
narrow, congested city streets. Thanks to a
combination of citizen effort, enlightened
planning, and responsible businessmen,
a public park (at right) tops five-story garage
of office complex in Oakland, California.

6

Youth, Education, and the Future

Our hope for the future lies in our children, far more than in ourselves. By 1985, a quarter of the families in the nation will be headed by children who are now in grade school or high school. They, and their older brothers and sisters, will soon form the new majority of voters, and they—not we—will then control the levers of power that determine our national priorities.

Beginning with the 1972 election year, youth becomes a political force to be reckoned with. Approximately 23 million young people between the ages of eighteen and twenty-four are eligible to vote for the first time in a presidential election. Eleven million of them, eighteen to twenty-one years of age, were enfranchised in 1971 by the 26th Amendment to the Constitution. In 1968, only about 73 million people went to the polls—62 percent of those who might have done so. If the same proportion of new voters cast ballots this year, there will be about 13 million additional votes to be tabulated. The potential importance of young voters is indicated by the fact that President Nixon had a popular majority of about 510,000 in 1968, and President Kennedy won by less than 120,000 votes in 1960.

Who, then, *are* these young people, and how well equipped are they for responsible citizenship? First of all, there is good support for the view that this is the best educated generation we have ever produced. Nearly 4 million youngsters now reach the age of eighteen each year and about three fourths—nearly 3 million—graduate from high school. (In 1940, only one of every four adults had completed high school.) Half of those who graduate from high school today—1.86 million—go on to college, and about half of these will stay in college until they graduate. In

229

1970, 16 percent of the age group between twenty-five and twenty-nine had completed four or more years of college. Only about 6 percent of this age group finished college in 1940.

These statistics are impressive in themselves, but they also give us a perspective on American youth which helps to counter the image projected by the radical minority. Campus riots and street demonstrations are news, but the overwhelming majority of young Americans have never been involved in any of them. In the first place, approximately 18 million of the 25.7 million young people now eighteen to twenty-four years old are not in college. Most of them are working, looking for work or serving in the armed forces. In the second place, even when student disorders were at their peak in the 1960s, it is estimated that no more than 20 percent of college students ever participated in any demonstrations at all. And very few even of these could be described as dedicated radicals. In 1969, the best known radical student organization—Students for a Democratic Society—had about 6,000 dues-paying members. From these figures, it becomes clear that—even in the 1960s—only a tiny minority of young Americans could be classified as extremists.

This does not mean, however, that the current young generation accepts without question the priorities and values which motivate their parents. Quite obviously, they do not. What it does mean is that American youth is not out to destroy our society and our institutions. Most of them (and, probably, most of their seniors) are not satisfied with things as they are, but they are willing to work within the system to modify our institutions and improve our society.

This fact provides some consolation to the beleaguered parents of today's youth, but it does little to bridge the generation gap. When sons or daughters emphatically reject parental values and accuse their elders of hypocrisy and materialism, a parent is bound to be both shaken and annoyed. Most of these parents were children of the depression of the 1930s, and many interrupted educations or careers to fight in World War II. That generation was not born to affluence and had neither the educational nor the vocational options open to the youth of today. If materialism was one of their vices, it was a materialism that launched, supported or enormously expanded social, educational, and humanitarian programs which are a model for the rest of the world. Some of the young dissidents of today appear to believe that they were the first to discover that injustice and inequality exist in this world, and the first to want to do something about it. But they are not starting from scratch. The revolution to which they subscribe was begun a long time ago by their parents. And it could be launched only because their grandparents and great-grandparents had developed a society that accepts criticism

230

Washington University, St. Louis, Missouri—campus church

Brandeis University,
Massachusetts—new graduate center

Montana State University
at Bozeman—field house

and welcomes change, and that provides the freedom and tolerance without which peaceful social progress cannot be achieved.

Americans have always believed—with an almost naive conviction —that education is the key to progress. As the frontier moved westward, the settlers began to build one-room schoolhouses. Later, as the nation's economy expanded, more and better schools were built. In the twelve months beginning in July of 1971, more than $85 billion will be spent on public and private education. This sum is about equal to the entire gross national product in 1938. In 1971-72 about 30 percent of the nation's population was enrolled in America's schools.

High school enrollment has increased by more than 50 percent in the past decade, and intensive efforts have been made to solve some of the pressing issues of the ghettos by improving the education of nonwhites. Between 1960 and 1970, the enrollment of nonwhites increased by 41 percent compared with an increase of 26 percent in the enrollment of whites. Most of this increase was in the country's 30,000 secondary schools and in the colleges. The increase for nonwhites in the secondary schools was 77 percent compared with nearly 40 percent for whites. And since 1968, black student enrollment at and above the college level has increased at a rate almost five times greater than the increase for whites.

In a truly pluralistic society, equality in education is a prerequisite for social and economic equality. But although the schools are of paramount importance in preparing our children to meet the responsibilities they will face in the future, the great youth groups that have been functioning in America for more than half a century also play a special role. Voluntary organizations in the familiar American pattern provide education in many fields outside the classroom, and inculcate virtues that are only incidentally a part of the school curriculum.

Innumerable church organizations flourish in every area, from parish or congregation to the national level. The Young Men's and Young Women's Christian Associations are outstanding, as are their Catholic and Jewish counterparts. The American Red Cross has a large junior organization and is engaged in many projects of community betterment, in addition to its well-known contributions to health care and training in life-saving. During the summer of 1971, hundreds of thousands of high school and college students volunteered to work with thousands of organizations. They ran day care centers, worked with drug addicts and the handicapped, promoted voter registration, taught swimming, arts and crafts to underprivileged children, practiced conservation in the national parks. There is no way to count the exact number of young volunteers, but the Red Cross estimates that it had more than 100,000 of them; some 27,000 students worked as classroom assistants for more than 500 summer Head Start programs; and countless thousands worked through private and religious agencies. One group of high school students spent seven weeks renovating and building houses for a black community in Louisiana; another built a meeting center for poor people in Maine; a third rebuilt adobe homes in New Mexico; a fourth built houses for mentally retarded children in Pennsylvania.

Then there are the 4.7 million Boy Scouts of America—one out of every four American boys eight to eighteen years of age. The Girl Scouts, with 3.2 million members, constitute 17 percent of girls seven to seventeen, and there are Camp Fire Girls—a smaller but similar group in a similar age bracket. In addition, there are 4 million or so boys and girls who pledge head, heart, hands, and health to clearer thinking, greater loyalty, larger service, and better living in the 4-H Clubs.

The size of these voluntary aggregations of young people is an indisputable sign of health among the youth of today, and of promise for the future. These groupings are not imposed by law, and have few of the economic and social pressures that exist in the processes of formal education. Their ideals are those of self-improvement and service to the community; their members are imbued with a deep sense of the value of the American heritage. They come together to learn specific skills and to have a good time. But they also learn—through contact with one another and with sympathetic older persons (more than 2 million adults work with Boy and Girl Scouts alone)—consideration for others, self-discipline, and the rewards of achievement through group endeavor.

The formal educational process is being extended to cover ever greater numbers of Americans, and to cover them for longer periods. It is going back from the kindergarten into preschool training, and beyond the bachelor's degree to advanced studies in the arts, the sciences, and the professions. Even the other most advanced countries in the world do not begin to offer the educational opportunities which are taken for granted in the United States. America's 1971-72 college population—about 8.4 million students—is three times as large as the college populations of all of Western Europe combined, although our total population is smaller. There are more nonwhites in our colleges than the *total* college population of any Western European country except France. And even in France, which leads Western Europe in college enrollment, education stops for most people at an early age. According to Jean-Francois Revel, a French author and journalist, "only one Frenchman in ten . . . finds it possible, economically, to advance beyond the equivalent of a grade-school education." In the United States, the median number of school years to which people over twenty-five had been exposed in 1970 was more than twelve—through high school and on into college.

Cub Scouts (above) help plant new trees on slope ravaged by California fire, and (at right) haul trash away to be recycled.

Cadette Scout (below) enjoys babysitting.

In purely practical terms, the more advanced America becomes technologically, the more extensive education must become in order to attain what is called "functional literacy"—which means the ability to read and understand, for instance, the rules of the road for motorists, or manuals for the operation of simple tools and appliances. The danger in so extensive a form of youth training, according to some of the doomsayers, is that the population may become "programmed" to certain life styles, and essential freedom of choice may be inhibited. But conscious programming of a mass educational system does not necessarily work over the long haul. It did not work, for example, in Hungary, where a generation educated under a lid of dogma revolted against that dogma.

Moreover, the American way of educating its youth is not a single system, but a complex of many systems. It developed, like nearly all of our institutions, by associative effort: a school here, an academy there, a university somewhere else—each reflecting the special needs and desires of some segment of the people. Public assistance to the school system began even before ratification of the Constitution—a lot in every township was authorized for a school by the Continental Congress in 1785—and has become increasingly more important in recent years. But the private sector has never been eliminated, nor the experimentation and cultural differences it encourages.

The private school system offers a variety of religious, social, and educational experience which serves the specially committed, the specially gifted, the specially handicapped—or the merely idiosyncratic. This prevents mass public education from ever becoming too complacent or too bureaucratic; it would be wrong to say that it leavens the lump, because the lump is yeasty enough. But just as voluntary hospitals can provide administrative and medical skills to improve mass health care, so private schools can pioneer methods and techniques which mass education may wish to use—or to avoid.

In America today, there are close to 1,500 private colleges and universities, and about 1,000 which are supported with public funds. Enrollment has almost tripled in the last twenty years, with 5.9 million in public institutions and 2.1 million in those which are privately funded. In the effort to accommodate the insistent flood of students, the universities have grown huge in size, complex and distant in administration. "Impersonality" was the chief complaint that sparked the 1964 riots on the Berkeley campus of the University of California, and impersonality is still a complaint of students in America's colleges and universities. But problems of size can be either cured or endured; they are not, of themselves, enough to explain the dissent and anger which have been prevalent on the nation's college campuses.

Although the overwhelming majority of colleges and college students have remained peaceful, there is no doubt that revolutionary changes are being discussed on campuses all over the country. *Fortune* once described students at the "quiet" universities as "a surprisingly sophisticated lot, far more concerned about world problems than their predecessors of even a few years ago, who used to run around in beanies and stage panty raids, and they have been better prepared by their high schools. They are more interested in learning to build new cities than in learning old theologies; and they want their universities to make them more intelligent, not more virtuous." Even though these students are not in the least interested in tearing down their universities or the nation's institutions, they—like the revolutionaries—are pressing for fundamental changes. They are more idealistic and more involved in the problems of society than any college generation since the 1930s.

It is difficult even to remember that in the 1950s and early 1960s Americans were almost as disturbed by what was called the "silent generation" as they are by the activists of today. College students then seemed to be alienated, apolitical, passive, and self-centered. Their cultural heroes were men like Jean-Paul Sartre, who preached the meaninglessness of human life, or the "beats" like Jack Kerouac. There was more poverty and more racial injustice in the 1950s than today, but most students simply were not interested.

What, then, brought the change in student attitudes that so suddenly became evident in the 1960s? There is no one answer to this question, but the pervasiveness of television coverage of the news has certainly been a factor. It was almost impossible, in the 1960s, to be indifferent while watching as fire hoses and attack dogs were used to disperse nonviolent demonstrations of blacks seeking equal rights. It was difficult to be unmoved when 200,000 people of every age and color gathered quietly in Washington in 1963 to petition for racial justice. And it has been a shattering experience for people of all ages to watch as young Americans fought, suffered, and died in the jungles of Vietnam.

Once upon a time, colleges and their students were isolated from the real world in the "ivory towers" of the world of education. But today this is no longer true. As more and more young people became actively involved in the struggle for racial equality and against poverty, in the effort to clean up the environment, and in demonstrations against the war, the quiet students watched, sympathized, and began to insist on rapid—though evolutionary—change.

One of the things that adults sometimes forget is that today's youth has grown up in a period of constant crises and accelerating change. They have developed a different sense of time, of how long it

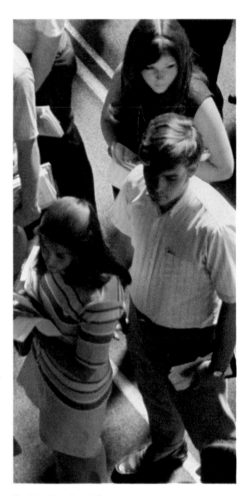

Registration day at the
University of Illinois at Urbana

234

takes to get things done. As children of the post-industrial, "technetronic" era, they are impatient and somewhat skeptical of the ability of their elders—and of our institutions—to adapt to the needs of the times. In a report made in 1970, Joseph L. Fisher, President of Resources for the Future, emphasized the problems that face us today:

"We in America are beset by a racial crisis, a youth crisis, a war crisis, an urban crisis, a population crisis, and an environmental crisis. By crisis I simply mean that a situation has become so bad that something has to be done about it, and done soon. . . .

"Perhaps what is involved in each is a recognition of the need for a more effective institutional response to new conditions than has been forthcoming thus far. The poor are uncertain as to whether governments and corporations can mount the programs required to assuage their problems. Minority ethnic groups are finding that laws and court decisions do not in themselves do enough to improve their lot. People everywhere have doubts that they can muster the self-discipline necessary for living in a congested, technological, urban society. The environmental crisis . . . raises similar doubts and uncertainties in the minds of everybody. Will the institutions of law and government, of industry and agriculture, of consumers and citizens be able to respond adequately to the forces that threaten our air, water, and land?

"In short, will the 'system' be able to deal with the crises promptly and constructively; will the 'establishment' that runs the numerous public and private organizations of the country succeed in staying on top of the problems? To this question the revolutionaries have their ready answer: tear the structure down, begin again. At the other extreme are an unreconstructed few who are content with things as they are. Most people, however, reject both these courses and would prefer to work with what exists, and reform it."

As a group, students tend to be more aware of social malaise—and to be in a better position to do something about it—than any other group. The psychologist, S. M. Lipset, argues that there is usually an increase in student activism "in periods in which belief in accepted verities of a society begins to break down, in which events undermine the stability and even the legitimacy of society's socio-economic arrangements, in which drastic social change occurs, or in which the political elite becomes sharply divided about the direction of policy." This seems to be such a period. In *The Conflict of Generations*, Dr. Lewis Feuer, the sociologist and educator, suggests that revolt of the young against the old is almost inevitable in any period, and that revolt turns to violence whenever the older generation loses its mantle of authority in the eyes of the young. As an example, Dr. Feuer says that if the ruling elders have made

The war in Vietnam—wounded soldier is rushed to evacuation helicopter during fighting on "Hamburger Hill."

Infantryman shouts warning (left) as sniper fire rakes encampment near Cambodian border.

Helicopter (below) brings in artillery piece as another is fired.

a mistake that has "major shameful consequences," they are likely to be regarded by the alert young as having lost their authority.

The war in Vietnam, in the eyes of most young people, seems to be viewed as just such a mistake. It was this bitterly unpopular war, more than any other influence, that mobilized youth from one end of the country to the other, uniting them in opposition as no other issue has ever done. The war has radicalized a few young people, and it has made skeptics of many others. Later the "elders," too, became disenchanted. A 1971 Harris poll showed that a majority of 60 as against 26 percent of the general public favored continuing troop withdrawals, whether the government of Saigon collapsed or not, and 58 as against 29 percent agreed that it was "morally wrong" for the United States to be fighting in Vietnam. This was a poll and not a referendum, of course, but it does indicate that many adult Americans have begun to feel as the young people do about this particular war.

Every young generation, as Dr. Feuer explained, tends to rebel against its elders, and one of the obvious ways to express this rebellion— to say "I'm different"—has always been with clothes and grooming. The current young generation, like the young people in the 1920s, has gone all out in this respect. Father went in for crew cuts and a close shave in the 1940's; his son may grow a beard and wear his hair somewhere between his shoulders and his waist. Father wore sober narrow ties, white shirts and dark suits; his son may wear jeans, wide, wildly patterned ties, gaudy shirts, and lime green jackets. In the 1940s, mother went in for permanent waves, short hair, dark red lipstick and mascara; her daughter wears her completely straight hair down to her waist and scorns makeup as "square." Mother wore spike heels, mid-calf skirts, a tight girdle, and an uplift bra; her daughter wears sandals, jeans or hot pants, and no bra at all. Fashions and hair styles probably started more individual family arguments than any other subject in the 1960s because it was a *specific* bone of contention between the generations. There were many other differences that worried and exasperated parents, but these were more subtle, harder to deal with, more difficult to express.

One of these was the revolution in sex mores, which has been enthusiastically promoted by young people all over the country. There is no doubt that Puritan America is fading. Adults are beginning to accept the fact that university dormitories are becoming co-educational, that anything goes on stage or screen, that girls of today—safeguarded by The Pill—are questioning the double standard of morality that was so much a part of their parents' world.

Adults who accept these changes do so reluctantly and with resignation. But they are not accepting the drug scene and all that goes with it. It has been estimated that 20 million Americans have at least experimented with marijuana and that the number of regular users could be anywhere from 400,000 to 3,000,000. Estimates indicate that perhaps 25 percent of students use amphetamines—pep pills—as study aids, and that about 200,000 people are addicted to heroin. About 25 percent of these addicts are probably under twenty-one.

There is great conflict between the generations on the subject of marijuana. Young people continue to press for legalizing its use on the grounds that it is not addictive. A great many of them feel strongly about this—their views were pretty cogently summarized by a student at the University of Chicago who denounced "the hypocrisies of an older generation that outlaws marijuana while drinking and smoking themselves to the grave." There is no doubt that alcoholism is a serious problem in our country. Some 80 million people drink regularly and six to nine million of them are alcoholics. Following heart disease, cancer, and mental illness, alcoholism can be considered the fourth major disease in America. The Department of Transportation estimates that one driver in every fifty is drunk, and that in 1970 more than 25,000 traffic deaths and 200,000 injuries involved drunk or drinking drivers. The cost to industry of alcoholism in absenteeism and accidents is estimated to be some $2 billion a year.

The campaign to "legalize pot" has broad support among the young. Even the 1971 White House Conference on Youth held at Estes Park in Colorado called for legalized sales under government regulation —though the delegates had been carefully chosen to be sure that radicals would not be over-represented. The arguments against legalization are that we do not yet know enough to be sure of the long range effects of smoking pot, and many people believe that it leads users toward experimenting with hard drugs. On the other side of the argument, there are those who believe that pot is harmless, does not lead to hard drugs, and that it would be better to take the sale out of the hands of criminal elements. This group also suggests that if pot were legal, rebellious youth might be less interested in smoking it.

It is not likely that pot smoking will be legalized in the near future because too many adults are afraid it is the first step toward the use of hard drugs. Because of this gut feeling, the generation gap is likely to continue in the drug area. Most adults believe that hard drugs are more dangerous than alcohol. The need to satisfy an addict's craving for heroin may make him turn to crime, but it is doubtful that even the heaviest drinker would be motivated to commit a serious crime in order to buy a bottle.

Drugs and music, for a time, seemed to be part and parcel of the

Co-ed dorms are now commonplace at
U.S. colleges and universities.
Above, student staff of an Oberlin
dorm get together in living room
of dorm director for Nepalese
dinner cooked by assistant dean of men.
Below, two members of junior class
study together in co-ed dorm room.

A sophomore at Oberlin College
in Ohio gets a free haircut.

youth culture. A 1967 Beatle album is filled with allusions to drugs, and many of the more recent favorites of the high school and college age group have been closely connected with the drug scene. Janis Joplin and Jimi Hendrix, called by many the king and queen of rock, packed in the youngsters—until both died of overdoses within a month of each other in 1970.

The music popularized by today's young generation, however, has been only incidentally drug oriented. Primarily, it reflects their life style and their idealism. Not for them the June and moon, love and dove, syndrome of a simpler era. For several years, when nonviolence was the watchword of black activists, students rode freedom buses and marched in civil rights protests singing "We Shall Overcome." Somewhat later, folk singers Bob Dylan and Joan Baez began a musical trend which combined entertainment with political involvement. Dylan suggested that the answers to our problems were "Blowin' in the Wind," and later the Jefferson Airplane popularized an antiwar song called "Volunteer."

James Taylor, one of the current favorites, is a modern-day troubador whose songs express the yearnings of many young people. In a recent album, "Sweet Baby James," he recorded several numbers reminiscent of the old Negro spirituals, reflecting something of a trend. The so-called "Jesus movement" has attracted many young people, and Billy Graham is beginning to believe that religion may be replacing the drug and sex themes of a few years ago. Attendance in established churches may be lagging, but thousands of youngsters—some of them former addicts—are travelling around the country spreading the gospel in their own way. A minister in California commented: "These kids still look like hippies but the change on the inside is miraculous." In liberal Catholic and Episcopal churches, the folk-rock mass is not uncommon. The exuberant rock opera, "Jesus Christ, Superstar," may appear to some adults to be almost sacrilegious, but they nevertheless recognize that it has generated enthusiasm and excitement. Through their musical contributions, youth infuses traditional religion with informality, warmth, and vitality.

Jimi Hendrix was one of rock's flamboyant superstars before his death, at 27, of an overdose of drugs in London.

During the 1960s, American youth questioned and challenged the basic values of our society. In the factories as well as in the universities, young people have made it clear that they resent the impersonal control of big business, big labor, and big government over their lives. They want a society which operates on a more human scale, a scale that permits more effective participation in decision making. They want a reordering of national priorities with more emphasis on the individual and on the quality of life, and less emphasis on creating an ever expanding market for gadgets they think we do not need. Many believe that the equal opportunity guaranteed by the Constitution is more myth than reality, and that one's place in society is too often preordained by birth and circumstance.

Janis Joplin, who died at 27 of a drug overdose, was completely exhausted at the end of a performance because she belted out her rock songs with such incredible energy.

The campuses of America have been quieter in the last year or two, but this does not mean that the rebellion is over. For the time being, at least, young people seem to believe that violence is not an effective instrument of change. There was revulsion among them when a graduate student at the University of Wisconsin was killed by a bomb explosion in a laboratory, and when amateur bomb-makers blew themselves up in Greenwich Village. The tragic killings at Kent State University and at Jackson State College shocked young people throughout the country—and reminded them that violence begets repression. "You aren't going to change the establishment with violence," is the way one youth put it to *U.S.News & World Report.*

There is a new type of activism on university campuses today. At the University of California at Santa Barbara, where a branch of the Bank of America was burned to the ground in 1970, the new activists are mature, intellectually sophisticated, and politically adroit. UCSB students are participating in a dialogue with the "establishment"—including representatives of business, university administrators, and political officials. The chairman of the board of the Bank of America, Louis B. Lundborg, whose institution contributed $25,000 for a Student Service Center, urged the community to understand the underlying causes for the bank burning. He recognized the need for protest, while differentiating between dissent and violence, and pointed out that young people are leading the nation toward the adoption of a new system of values which we cannot simply ignore. They are challenging the "establishment" to prove its flexibility and its ability to accommodate change, and they are questioning the values and attitudes that both reflect and shape the society as a whole. They are asking questions about poverty, urban blight, discrimination, the destruction of the environment.

These and many other fundamental issues which will affect the future of our country are being raised by intelligent and well-educated young people who are looking with fresh eyes at the world around them. "The essential message I get from the protest and the turmoil among today's young people," Henry Ford II observed, "is that they do care enough to insist on something better. My generation is rightly dismayed by their intemperance, their impatience, and their occasional violence. But we must also confess that they might be more reasonable if we had been more responsible."

Adult Americans have thought a great deal about responsibility in recent years, and have begun themselves to question some of the basic assumptions which their children have been challenging so insistently. How effective, for instance, is presidential leadership? What can we do to improve the efficiency of our court system? What about the integrity and responsiveness of Congress? What can be done to reduce and streamline the bureaucracy? What about the social responsibility of business? Are local governments competent to run the schools, police the streets, collect the garbage? Does the "system" work, in other words, and if it doesn't work well enough, how can it be made to work better?

There are also indications today that the older generation—like the young—is beginning to adopt a different set of values. They are still interested in material well-being and will work to achieve it. But material comfort and competitive "success" are no longer ends in themselves, except for the small minority that can still be classified as poor. Perhaps because the economy is now capable of taking care of all the needs of every segment of the population—an impressive achievement in itself—more and more people are beginning to press for changes that would have been considered utopian a few short years ago.

The generation gap still exists, as it always has, but at the moment it seems to be narrowing. On the campuses, administrators and faculty have made greater efforts to respond to the valid complaints of their students, and students in turn are behaving more responsibly. In the factories, management is thinking about esoteric things like job satisfaction, and beginning to experiment with new work schedules and more concentrated work weeks. Now that so many adults have joined the young in opposition to the Vietnam war, this tragic issue is less divisive. Dress and hair styles no longer seem to be as important, perhaps because most people realize that such fads do not last forever. Although the young are somewhat skeptical, most are working within the political system to implement change at the polls—in the traditional American way. The ablest graduates of business and law schools are working inside the "establishment," using their considerable drive and influence to accelerate the movement toward social responsibility on the part of business.

In spite of all the talk about young people who reject the work

College students conducted registration campaigns, and new young voters all over the country are now hard at work for favorite candidates.

ethic and believe that it is somehow more moral to be poor than to be rich, the overwhelming majority is willing to work hard. They expect to be well paid for their work, and many of them also expect their work to contribute something to the quality of our society. The best of our young people are idealists, as their parents and grandparents were before them. They do not seem to be much interested in how far we have come to get where we are. What matters to them is where we are going and how we will get there.

This, in the final analysis, is what has mattered most to every young generation of Americans. For those who came of age in a simpler era, there was always a new world waiting to be built out on the western frontier. But the challenge today is both more subtle and more complex. It calls for young people who have the imagination, the brains, and the will to delineate and dramatize the problems that face us. The current young generation has been doing exactly that for most of the last decade. They have also demonstrated that, like their forbears, they have the courage of their convictions, and the vigor to adapt our democratic institutions to the pressing needs of our time.

There is continuity here, for this is what America has been all about since the first settlers dropped anchor at Jamestown and Plymouth.

They care enough to insist on something better

Young Americans do not know whether or not they will be
effective in their efforts to improve our society, but the best
of them certainly intend to try. Many are already in the business
world, pressing their employers to assume more responsibility and
to play a more creative role in solving the problems that face us.
Others, like the intent young students shown on these pages, are
willing to listen as well as to talk to representatives of leading
corporations like Prudential Insurance and Eastman Kodak.

Symposium at Gettysburg College in Pennsylvania featured leading American businessmen as well as frequent critics of business. Corporate recruiters, sometimes harassed in the 1960s, are being treated with more respect in the 1970s.

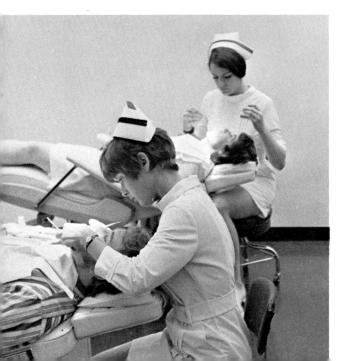

Trades and marketable skills are learned by many young
people who are not particularly interested in a liberal arts education.
The farm boy feeding his calves at left may study the modern
science of agriculture if he goes to college. The second-year dental
hygiene students (below, left) at Forest Park Community College
in St. Louis are cleaning the teeth of patients at the clinic.
They can earn a starting salary of $700 a month, once they finish
their two-year course and pass the state exams for licensed hygienists.
The somewhat startled youngster with the blowtorch may eventually
earn a good living as a welder, and the young carpenters working on
a North Carolina bridge (below) are well on their way to good jobs
in the construction industry.

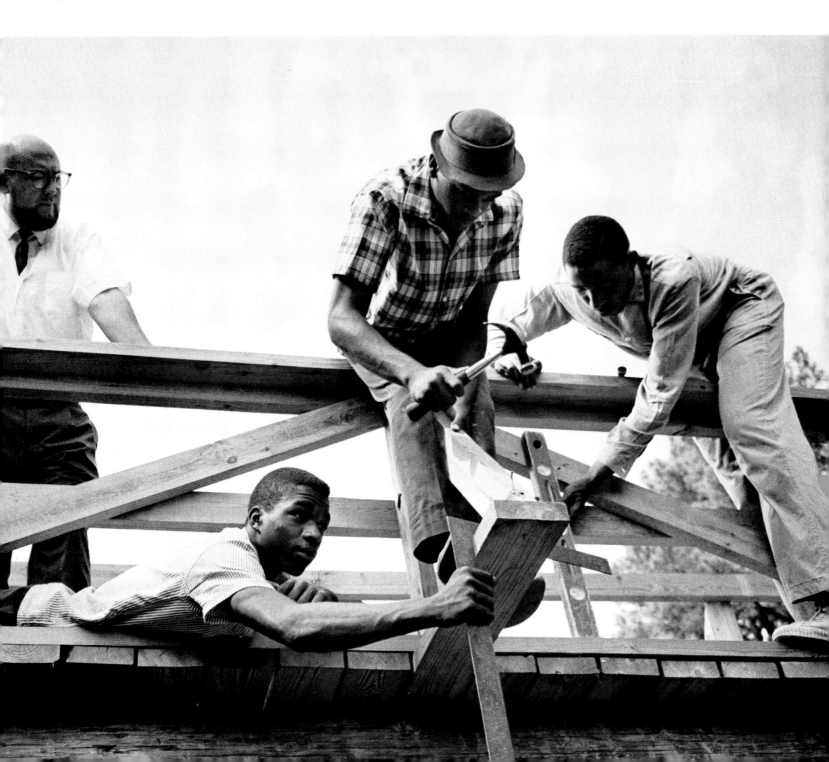

They gathered together in hundreds of thousands to
listen to the amplified rock music of others. And they also
went off alone, to think about life and to play quietly on their
guitars—for the wind and the waves, or just for themselves.
In 1969, more than 400,000 young people swarmed over a rented,
600-acre farm near Woodstock in the Catskill Mountains of New York.
It was the greatest rock festival ever held, and those who were there
will never forget it. But even two years later, such festivals
were out of style. The craving of the young for peaceful
moments by themselves—with or without guitar—is something,
however, that doesn't change from one generation to the next.

The Leapwood Avenu
Elementary School
near Los Angeles was
white 9 years ago.
Today (right) it is
perfectly integrated.
Social attitudes
change slowly and
there are many
problems, but
progress is being
made everywhere.

The beginning, for a shy little girl with a great big satchel, is a schoolroom where she will learn to understand some of the mysteries contained on shelves of books. What she—and 44 million other schoolchildren between the ages of 3 and 13—will be able to do with her life is in large part determined by the quality of the education she receives in the early school years. This, for America, is where the future begins.

Good teachers mean more to education than every *thing* a school system can provide. They know when to help a puzzled youngster like the one at left; they know how to make a boy's eyes light up with excited understanding; they know how much a congratulatory handshake can mean.

Second graders at demonstration school in Rockford, Illinois, dress up for year-end play. Their 24-year-old intern-teacher used unconventional methods, his pupils did well—and loved every minute of it.

Cheerful classrooms, up-to-date equipment, plenty of books, and a handsome gym that converts into a cafeteria—these are some of the things that encourage children to enjoy the process of learning. Taxpayers sometimes grumble, but were willing to spend an estimated $44 billion on public schools in 1971.

Lincoln Elementary School (left) in Columbus, Indiana

Public Library in Skokie, Illinois, runs special preschool classes.

C.C. Lambert Elementary School in Tustin, California

Nearly 15 million young people are enrolled in U.S. high schools, an increase of 43.6 percent in the last decade. About 1.2 million are attending private schools. In an effort to improve the quality of education, many cities have at least one experimental program where curriculum and teaching techniques are unorthodox but stimulating to the students. One of these, Philadelphia's Parkway Program—partially funded by a grant from the Ford Foundation—is shown below during a regular weekly meeting between students and faculty to discuss problems and future plans.

Typing class in a public school in Cleveland, Ohio

Young teacher in Atlanta, Ga. gets the concentrated attention of her class.

Religious faith is still a part of the lives of our young people, no matter where or how they are taught to worship. Parents take their children to church on Sundays, and little girls like those at far left learn to say grace before eating—at a day care center in Blanchard, Pennsylvania. For a pair of teenage boys in Cleveland, Ohio, a contribution to the local church is to vacuum its floors in preparation for Sunday services.

THIS DO IN REMEMBRANCE OF ME

The war in Vietnam—a bitterly divisive issue—brought thousands of young people into the streets for marches and demonstrations. As American troops withdraw, the tension lessens, but there is very little doubt that most of the younger generation opposes war unless the safety of this country is directly threatened.

"March Against Death", in 1969, went on day and night for 40 hours, as 50,000 people walked silently from Arlington National Cemetery to put the names of American soldiers who died in Vietnam into coffins placed below the U.S. Capitol.

Youth takes the admonition on the sign below very seriously. It was carried during a 1971 peace march in San Francisco.

Only one person can end the war.

You.

Veterans returned from Vietnam protest the war by joining a Washington demonstration in April of 1971.

The peace sign popularized by young Americans floats over more than 100,000 who gathered in Boston Common (below) on Moratorium Day in 1969.

The tragedy of drug addiction is written on the face
of Chad Harris, a veteran wounded at Khesanh who became hooked on
a variety of drugs while moving from hospital to hospital in Vietnam.
He became addicted to heroin after his discharge, was able to get into
the drug treatment center at the Palo Alto Veterans Administration
Hospital in California. Chad has been off heroin ever since and
is now on methadone maintenance, which is used to buy time until
researchers can find something better, or until the patient can be
weaned from dependence on any drug. Possibly the most important
part of Chad's treatment is in regular group and other kinds of therapy
sessions that help a man to face his addiction, and to find out how
to handle underlying problems. Methadone, Chad says, is "a crutch
I'll use for a while. But some day I'll walk free."

The tears running down Chad's cheeks are partly the result of 14 hours without a fix, partly fear that he will not be one of the lucky few admitted into this particular program.

Simply talking with group therapist Jewel Barnes (right) is part of Chad's therapy.

Debi, Chad's young wife, moved to the San Francisco area so she and the baby could be with him every day.

Motorbike riding was popularized by the young, who like the ear-splitting noise, the speed and sense of adventure it provides. The cost factor is also an inducement, since a motorcycle is cheaper than a car to buy and to operate. Many adults have also entered the market —probably for the same reasons. At left, 605 cyclists race 75 miles across the dust of California's Mojave Desert. The intrepid racers shown below are bouncing up a rough trail in a Massachusetts ski area.

The Boy Scouts are moving into the inner cities, with programs that are relevant to youngsters who may never have a chance to go on overnight hikes along a country trail—and who don't need much information about snake-bite remedies, but ought to know what to do about a rat bite. Although only about 16 percent of eligible urban boys join, compared with 25 percent of boys who live elsewhere, the gap is closing as scouting confronts the realities of the 1970s.

Shaggy hair is permitted in New York City's Troop 35.

Urban camping on a vacant lot in Milwaukee makes sense for the city kids who don't often get a trip to the country.

Firelight camaraderie in a south Bronx church is as meaningful as it would be with a log fire under the stars.

Working for constructive causes probably involves
more young people today than ever before. Some of these causes
are national in scope, others concern matters of strictly local
interest. One example is the demonstration below. With homemade
signs, high school students petition the Governor of Rhode Island
to continue "Project Discovery," a cultural program involving
a local repertory company with local schools.

In New Haven, Conn., a Yale student working against the population explosion turns his bathroom into a print shop for ZPG posters.

Hikes to raise money for the poor and sick were held in over 200 cities in 1971. Money was pledged in advance on a per-mile basis. In Rochester, N.Y. (left and above), 32,000 people walked 750,000 miles to earn $600,000—plus 64,000 sore feet.

Earth Day in 1970 brought out hundreds of thousands all over the country. The rally below is at Washington Monument.

The "Jesus Movement" has become something of a crusade to thousands of young people. It is nondenominational, and resembles old-time, fundamentalist revivals much more than the restrained services held in most churches today. And—above all—it is joyous! It may be a fad or, as one minister put it, it may be "the greatest awakening in the history of the church."

Teenager in California gives the "Jesus sign."

Movement symbol

Singing and clapping hands,
these converts to the movement
voice their faith in Jesus.

Prayer-and-fellowship meeting in Rye, N.Y., features Bible reading.
Most of those in the movement are in their teens or early twenties.

271

Beautiful school buildings have been going up all over
the country for years. In 1970 alone—which was by no means
a record year—educational buildings valued at more than $6.3 billion were
put in place. $745 million of this total went into private educational facilities.
The remainder, representing more than half the value of new construction
of all public buildings in 1970, went into public schools and colleges.

Hillspoint Elementary
School, Westport,
Conn.

Library of the University of California, San Diego (left)

Canada College, a two-year community college in Redwood City, Cal.

Potential voters, who once rejected "the system," began to enroll in it when they registered to vote in the fall of 1971. A few of them wear ratty clothes, long hair, and beards, but their efforts to register themselves and each other indicate that they are willing to work for change in the traditional way. How many will actually vote is impossible to predict, but if they vote in substantial numbers it will prove that this generation is no more "alienated" than any other.

Penn State students outnumber townspeople 4 to 1. Local mayor (left) talks
things over at information table for students who want to register and vote.

Pollution is not a real problem.

Let them register,
next thing you know
they'll be voting.

Youth Citizenship Fund headquarters
in Washington, D.C. (above) coordinates
bipartisan registration drives across
the country.

More than 4,000 took the oath (left) and
were registered during a Pittsburgh rally.

Young matron is registered on the streets of Los Angeles
by an 18-year-old volunteer registrar.

"Women's Lib" is a new name for an ancient cause. The current drive for full equality calls for many of the same rights sought by the Women's Rights Convention of 1848. Although the actions and rhetoric of a few of the feminists seem somewhat extreme, great inequities still exist, and there is little doubt about the justice of their cause.

From generation to generation, some things never change.
Young people still find solitude in a drifting rowboat, brightening
the water with the reflected color of gay balloons. When they're very
young, some of them still play cat's cradle with an old piece of string.
Others—completely oblivious to the brooding photograph of Albert Einstein
behind them—"relate" to each other with a shared and joyous laugh.
They still spend hours, too, sitting close together on the grass,
talking of love and life—and of their hopes for the future.

We have much more in common with each other than we think, and we are getting together to change the things that need to be changed. Ever since they were born, we have been telling our children what we ourselves have learned. It is only fitting—as they grow up—that they tell us something of what *they* have learned, and share with us their vision of a future that they, with our help, must build.

Picture Credits

*Credits from left to right
are separated by semicolons, from
top to bottom by dashes.*

8 Guy Gillette **9** Declan Haun, Black Star; Mary Ellen Mark, Magnum; Laszlo L. Kondor—Burk Uzzle, Magnum(2)

Chapter One.

10-11 Grant Heilman **12-13** Arthur Griffin; Robert Wenkam **14-15** Philip Hyde—Ed Cooper; Philip Hyde, by permission of the Sierra Club **16-17** Ed Cooper **18-19** Grant Heilman—H. Stanley Johnson, FPG; Grant Heilman **20** Grant Heilman **21** Ed Cooper **22-23** Esther Henderson, Rapho Guillumette—David Muench—Ernst Haas, Magnum **24-25** Esther Henderson, Rapho Guillumette **26** David Muench **28-29** Ansel Adams **30-31** Charles Harbutt, Magnum—Elliott Erwitt, Magnum **32** Elliott Erwitt, Magnum **33** UPI **34-35** Richard Swartz(1) Bruce McAllister, Black Star(3) Cynthia Johnston(4) Maria Ealand (7) Ellen K. Wright(1) **36-37** Tom Hollyman, Photo Researchers **38-39** Eberhart Studio— Warren K. Leffler, USN&WR—Sal Crisanti; Wide World **40-41** Flip Schulke, Black Star—UPI; UPI **43** Robert Lautman **44** Arthur Griffin **45** Mary Eleanor Browning, DPI **46-47** U.S. Dept. of Agri.; A. Aubrey Bodine **48-49** Andreas Feininger; Margaret Durrance—Chicago Ass. Com. Ind. **50-51** Charles Rotkin, from *The U.S.A.; Roy Hankey*

Chapter Two.

52 Burk Uzzle, Magnum **54** Lee Balterman, *LIFE* © Time Inc.—Arthur Rickerby, *LIFE* © Time Inc.—El Paso Natural Gas **55** Grant Heilman **56-57** Warren K. Leffler, USN&WR **58** NASA **59** Ralph Crane, *LIFE* © Time Inc. **60-61** Gerald Martineau, *The Washington Post* **62-63** John Launois, Black Star **64-65** David Attie; courtesy ITT—courtesy Xerox Corp.—courtesy Eastman Kodak Co. **66-67** Paul Conklin(5) Maria Ealand(2) Marion S. Trikosko, USN&WR(1) **68-69** © 1971 by Jon Erikson from *The Middle Americans* **70-71** John Launois, Black Star **72-73** courtesy General Motors exc. (ctr) John Launois, Black Star **74-75** John Launois, Black Star **76** Grant Heilman **77** Burk Uzzle, Magnum—Bradley Smith, New York **78-79** American Airlines—Alfred Eisenstaedt; (rt) Grant Heilman **80-81** John Dominis, *LIFE* © Time Inc. **82-83** Joe Munroe, Photo Researchers(2); (rt) El Paso Natural Gas **84** Charles Rotkin, from *The U.S.A.* **85** Yale Joel, *LIFE* © Time Inc. (2)—Yankee Atomic Electric Co. **86-87** Chuck Rogers, Black Star—Union Oil Co. of Calif.; Yale Joel, *LIFE* © Time Inc. **88-89** courtesy United Airlines; A. Aubrey Bodine; Erich Hartmann, Magnum—David Plowden, *The Hand of Man on America,* Smithsonian Institution Press **90** John Bryson, Rapho Guillumette **91** M.E. Warren, Photo Researchers; (top) Jay Maisel, courtesy AT&T—(bot) Wayne Miller, Magnum **92** Jay Maisel, courtesy AT&T **93** Shel Hershorn, Black Star; Steve

Schapiro, Black Star—(bot) Jay Maisel, courtesy AT&T; Ken Heyman **94** Ken Heyman **95** courtesy General Motors **96-97** John Launois, Black Star exc. (bot.lf) Joe Brenneis **98-99** NASA exc. (ctr.rt) © 1971 by Jon Erikson from *The Middle Americans* **100-101** Tom Tracy; Bruce Davidson, Magnum— courtesy Westinghouse Electric Corp.; Joseph Sterling **102** J.R. Eyerman **103** Curt Gunther, Camera 5 **104-105** John Dominis, *LIFE* © Time Inc.; Robert Burroughs—Elliott Erwitt, Magnum **106** J. Alexander, Fred Figall, D.C. Redevelopment Land Agency(2); Robert Perron, Photo Researchers **107** Burk Uzzle, Magnum

Chapter Three.

108 Leonard McCombe, *LIFE* © Time Inc. —Ken Heyman **110** Frank Hoy **112-113** Great Northern Railway Photo—USN&WR —courtesy Schwinn Bicycle Co. **114** Albert Fenn **115** © Walt Disney Productions **116-117** Ron Lerner, *LOOK* **118** Allan Matthews, Georgia Dept. of Ind. & Tr.; Ernie Day—(bot) Douglas Kirkland, *LOOK* **119** John Dominis, *LIFE* © Time Inc.; Ken Heyman **120-121** Leslie Todd; John Loengard, *LIFE* © Time Inc. **122-123** A.Y. Owen—Ralph Crane, *LIFE* © Time Inc.(2) **124** Bill Eppridge; Arthur Rickerby, *LIFE* © Time Inc. (2)—Paul Seaman **125** Douglas Rodrick **126-127** Les Blacklock—David Muench; (ctr) Winston Pote; Les Blacklock **128** William J. Stravitz—Alfred Eisenstaedt **129** Frank Gordon **130-131** Paul Conklin; Burk Uzzle, Magnum; (top rt) *Hamilton County* © 1970 by McKinley & Tim Kantor—Tom Hollyman, Photo Researchers—Paul Conklin **132** *Hamilton County* © 1970 by McKinley & Tim Kantor **133** Elliott Erwitt —Burk Uzzle, Magnum(2) **134-135** Michael A. Vaccaro, *LOOK;* (top) Robert Wenkam, by permission of the Sierra Club—Burk Uzzle, Magnum, *LIFE* © Time Inc. **136-137** *SPORTS ILLUSTRATED,* Neil Leifer © Time Inc.—(top) LeRoy Grannis; Luis Melendez, Globe Photos—Ed Cooper **138-139** Margaret Durrance **140-141** Margaret Durrance(2); (bot) Winston Pote; (rt) *Hamilton County* © 1970 by McKinley and Tim Kantor **142-143** *SPORTS ILLUSTRATED* © Time Inc. photos by Sheedy & Long; Walter Iooss(2)—(bot) Lane Stewart **144** William S. Keller, Nat. Park Service **145** David Muench; (top) C.G. Maxwell— Vivienne, Photo Researchers(2)— *Hamilton County* © 1970 by McKinley and Tim Kantor **146-147** Nancy J. Butler by permission of the Sierra Club— Margaret Durrance; (ctr and top) Retta Johnston, by permission of the Sierra Club(2)—Margaret Durrance **148-149** Douglas Kirkland, *LOOK*—Gary Gladstone from *Hey, Hey Can't Catch Me* **150** Kosti Ruohomaa, Black Star—Ed Judice, courtesy Stan. Oil N.J. **151** Retta Johnston, by permission of the Sierra Club

Chapter Four.

152-153 Eric Schaal © Time Inc.— Elliott Landy, Magnum—Martha Swope; (rt) Wayne Miller—David Hurn, Magnum (2)—M.E. Warren, Photo Researchers **154-155** Joe Baldwin, *LOOK*—Elliott Landy, Magnum **156-157** Jack Mitchell —Ernst Haas, Magnum **158-159** Charlotte Brooks, *LOOK;* John Dominis, *LIFE* © Time Inc.—(ctr) New York Production *Hair;* (rt) Bruce Davidson, Magnum **160-161** Metropolitan Museum of Art; National Gallery of Art, Washington, D.C. —Maria Ealand **162-163** Peter Costas **164-165** Ezra Stoller, courtesy Lever Brothers—courtesy S.C. Johnson & Son, Inc.; Sergio Larrain, Magnum **166-167** Dennis Stock, Magnum(2)—Don Haynes from *Great Dance Bands* by L. Walker **168-169** Peter Costas **170-171** Fletcher Drake, The Kennedy Center for the Performing Arts—Stan Wayman, *LIFE* © Time Inc. **172** Andreas Feininger **173** Paul Conklin—David Hurn, Magnum—Margaret Durrance **174-175** David Hurn, Magnum; M.E. Warren, Photo Researchers **176-177** Burt Glinn; Dennis Stock, Magnum(2); (top) Vincent Nanfra, *LOOK* **178-179** Burk Uzzle, Magnum (top) Young Audiences, Inc.; Carl Purcell, NEA(2) **180** Gjon Mili, *LIFE* © Time Inc. **181** Bill Eppridge— Henry Groskinsky, *LIFE* © Time Inc.(2) **182** David Hurn, Magnum—Dan Budnick **183** Ken Heyman—Carl Purcell, NEA **184-185** Ezra Stoller—Balthazar Korab; Jane Doggett and Malcolm Smith **186-187** Michael Rougier—Henry Groskinsky, *LIFE* © Time Inc.(2) **188-189** Constantine Manos, Magnum **190** (top) Dennis Stock, Magnum—Jay Maisel **191** Jack Lind; (top) Raymond Lustig—Robert Parent **192-193** Ed Cooper; Arthur Griffin; (top) Robert Lautman

Chapter Five.

194 Chris Springman, Black Star(2); (rt) George Silk, *LIFE* © Time Inc. **196-197** courtesy March of Dimes—Paul Conklin, VISTA **198-199** Paul Conklin, Teachers Corps.—Nat. Oceanic and Atmos. Adm.—Ray Palmer, Red Cross **200** Morton R. Engelberg, Headstart— James Foote, VISTA **201** Morton R. Engelberg, Headstart **202-203** George de Vincent—Katrina Thomas, Photo Researchers **204-205** Arthur Schatz, *LIFE* © Time Inc.; Marion S. Trikosko, USN&WR—Arthur Schatz, *LIFE* © Time Inc. **206-207** Dennis Brack, Black Star; Leonard McCombe, *LIFE* © Time Inc.—David Plowden, *The Hand of Man on America,* Smithsonian Institution Press **208-209** Burton Berinsky, Black Star—League of Women Voters—Wide World **210-211** Paul Conklin—Rowland Scherman, Peace Corps(2)—(bot and rt) courtesy CARE **212-213** Linda Wheeler, *The Washington Post;* Ralph Morse, *LIFE* © Time Inc.; Winston Vargas, Photo Researchers **214-215** Ralph Crane, *LIFE* © Time Inc. —David Plowden, *The Hand of Man on America,* Smithsonian Institution Press;

Dept. of Lighting, Seattle, Wash.(2) **216-217** Joel Peter Witkin, City Walls, Inc.(2); George Silk, *LIFE* © Time Inc. **218** Paul Conklin—Richard L. Stack, Black Star; Aero Service Corp., Division of Litton Indus. **219** Gene Daniels, Black Star—Charles Okamura, *Honolulu Advertiser* **220** Jan Mason, *LIFE* © Time Inc. **221** Roger Mallock, Magnum—David Plowden **222-223** Charles Rotkin from *The U.S.A.;* Ralph Crane, *LIFE* © Time Inc.(3) **224-225** Ralph Crane, *LIFE* © Time Inc. (4); Elliot Erwitt, Magnum **226** Marathon Oil Co.; D. Gorton, *N.Y. Times* —(bot) *N.Y. Daily News* **227** courtesy Kaiser Industries Corp.

Chapter Six.

228 Vernon Merritt III, *LIFE* © Time Inc. **230-231** W.A. Howe, FPG—Jack Zhert— Carlos Elmer, Alpha(2) **232-233** John Schearer, *LIFE* © Time Inc.—John Vachon, *LOOK*—(bot) courtesy Girl Scouts of America **234-235** Lee Balterman **236-237** Wide World; UPI—Wide World **238-239** Bill Ray, *LIFE* © Time Inc. **240-241** Tucker Ransom, Pictorial Parade —Elliott Landy, Magnum **242-243** Matthew Lewis—Charles Del Vecchio *The Washington Post*(2); Andy Sachs, *N.Y. Times* **244-245** Yoichi R. Okamoto **246-247** Paul Conklin—Larry Kuban, The Junior College District of St. Louis; Wayne Miller, Magnum; Ken Heyman **248-249** John Dominis, *LIFE* © Time Inc. —Jerry Russell by permission of the Sierra Club **250** James Foote, OEO **251** Thomas Koeniges, *LOOK*—Ralph Crane, *LIFE* © Time Inc. **252-253** Bruce Roberts, Rapho Guillumette; NEA; George Bettridge, PIX—(bot) Tod Tarbox **254** Orlando Cabanban, Gunnar Birkerts Assoc. **255** NEA; Bruce Beck—William Blurock & Partners **256-257** Arthur Schatz, *LIFE* © Time Inc.; John Marshall Tyle—Tom J. O'Halloran, USN&WR **258** George Silk, *LIFE* © Time Inc. **259** Maria Ealand—Burk Uzzle, Magnum **260-261** Stanley Tretick, *LOOK*—Ben Tarcher, Black Star; M. Abramson, Black Star— Yale Joel, *LIFE* © Time Inc. **262-263** Arthur Schatz, *LIFE* © Time Inc. **264-265** Bill Eppridge, *LIFE* © Time Inc; © 1971 by Jon Erikson from *The Middle Americans* **266-267** John Schearer, *LIFE* © Time Inc. **268** courtesy Trinity Square Repertory Co. **269** Arthur Rickerby— (ctr and rt) Arthur Schatz, *LIFE* © Time Inc.(3)—*The Washington Post* **270-271** Julian Wasser; Jack and Betty Cheetham, Bethel(2)—(bot) Vernon Merritt III, *LIFE* © Time Inc. **272-273** J.R. Eyerman(2); (top) NEA **274-275** Harry Benson, *LIFE* © Time Inc. **276** Mary Ellen Mark, Woodfin Camp, Inc.—John Olson, *LIFE* © Time Inc. **277** Wide World **278** Retta Johnston, by permission of the Sierra Club **279** David Bitts, *LIFE* © Time Inc.; Wayne Miller, Magnum—Don Getsug, Rapho Guillumette **280-281** J.R. Eyerman; Mike Mauney, *LIFE* © Time Inc.—Van Bucher, Photo Researchers; Stanley Tretick, *LOOK*

Index